# REAL
# ESTATE
# RESCUE

# REAL
# ESTATE
# RESCUE

## HOW AMERICA LEAVES BILLIONS BEHIND IN RESIDENTIAL REAL ESTATE AND HOW TO MAXIMIZE YOUR HOME'S VALUE

TRACY MCLAUGHLIN

with Kevin Lake

CORAL GABLES

Published by Mango Publishing Group, a division of Mango Media Inc.

Cover: © Jennifer K. Beal Davis
Layout & Design: Morgane Leoni
Illustrations: © Laura Baran
Photo page 136: © Judy Meuschke Compass

For permission requests, please contact the publisher at:
Mango Publishing Group
2850 S Douglas Road, 2nd Floor
Coral Gables, FL 33134 USA
info@mango.bz

For special orders, quantity sales, course adoptions and corporate sales, please email the publisher at sales@mango.bz. For trade and wholesale sales, please contact Ingram Publisher Services at customer.service@ingramcontent.com or +1.800.509.4887.

Real Estate Rescue: How America Leaves Billions Behind in Residential Real Estate and How to Maximize Your Home's Value

Library of Congress Cataloging-in-Publication number: 2019954731
ISBN: (print) 978-1-64250-195-7, (ebook) 978-1-64250-196-4
BISAC category code BUS054010—BUSINESS & ECONOMICS / Real Estate / Buying & Selling Homes

Printed in the United States of America

For Lorna Hines, one of the truly great real estate minds in the country, and my three children, Ross, Whitney, and Grace.

# Contents

Introduction      9
**Wake Up America!**

     Trust Is Earned      11
     The Bind      16

Chapter 1      19
**There Are No Picassos in Real Estate–Valuing a Home**

     The Mechanics of Home Valuation      22
     The Art of Home Valuation      24
     An Appraisal of the Appraisal      37

Chapter 2      41
**The Price Better Be Right**

     Going, Going, Gone      44
     The Golden Days      48
     Price Reductions—Don't Burn the Clock      49
     The Anchor Bias      50
     Winter, Spring, Summer, or Fall: When to Sell Your Home      52

Chapter 3      54
**Preparing a Home for Sale**

     The Times They Are a-Changin'      55
     Home Sweet Home      58
     Feeling Misunderstood and Depreciated      59
     A Broken Clock Is Right Twice a Day: Timing the Market      61
     Condition of the Home      62
     Know Thy Market      63
     Detailing Design Changes for a Seller      66
     Time for "The Talk"      66
     Staging—Showing Buyers How to Live in a Home      68

## Chapter 4     74
**Two Pictures (Before & After) Say a Thousand Words**

Case Study 1: Get Creative    76
Case Study 2: Empty Homes Are Houses    81
Case Study 3: Shingle-Style Residence    85
Case Study 4: Waterfront Residence    89
Case Study 5: Repositioning an East Coast Home on the West Coast    93
Case Study 6: San Francisco Townhome    96

## Chapter 5     106
**Disclose, Permit, Inspect**

In the Interest of Full Disclosure    108
Permits    110
Pre-Listing Inspections    113

## Chapter 6     116
**Marketing and Branding a Home**

Storytelling    119
I Feel Therefore I Buy: Emotions Drive Decision-Making    122
Branding Tools    125
Social Media and Property Voyeurism    126

## Chapter 7     129
**Buyer Be Aware**

The Neighbors, Not the Numbers, Tell the Story    132
The Good, the Bad, and the Ugly    133
Yabba Dabba Don't    136
The Titanic Was "Unsinkable": Prepare for the Unexpected    137
Your Home Is Not an ATM    139

## Chapter 8     143
**Didn't Aunt Louise Just Get Licensed? Finding the Right Agent**

Driving Away with Tears in My Eyes    144
VCRs, Pay Phones, Real Estate Agents?    147
Do Due Diligence    148

Go Local                                                              153
I Hope the Friendship Was Worth Half a Million Dollars               154
Buying a Listing                                                     157
A Punch List: Questions to Ask a Prospective Agent                   159

**Chapter 9**                                                        161
**Buying and Selling Homes: What the Future Looks Like**

Money Talks                                                          162
Artificial Intelligence                                              163
The Millennial Mindset                                               163
The Traditional Brokerage—Calling a Taxi to Take You to Blockbuster  166
The Brokerage of the Future                                          168

**About the Author**                                                 173

**Endnotes**                                                         176

# Introduction

# WAKE UP AMERICA!

If you've ever bought or sold a home, you likely left money on the table. And I don't mean that the escrow company left you with the FedEx bill for the closing papers. In almost every real estate sale, buyers and sellers leave behind thousands or hundreds of thousands of dollars in the process, depending on the home values in your market. Given that the typical American homeowner has 40 percent of their wealth tied up in their home,[1] the financial consequences can impact you for decades to come.

The good news? You will never know how much money you left on the table. If ignorance is bliss, American home buyers and sellers should be in a state of rapture. Every day, I watch buyers and sellers make well-intentioned but ill-informed decisions that undermine the monetization of their asset. Their decision-making processes are guided by a vague understanding of the real estate business, gut instinct, and, to varying degrees, the advice of their representatives. They have little awareness that their seemingly innocuous choices ripple out into all aspects of the sales process with extraordinary costs to them.

Residential real estate commands a great deal of attention in our culture, yet there has been no clear road map for buyers and sellers to maximize the value of the sale and purchase of homes—until now. This book will change your understanding of how to buy and sell a home. I'm going to show you, step by step, a strategic and comprehensive approach to buying and selling homes that guarantees you will NOT leave money on the table.

I've been the number-one producer in residential sales in Marin County, California, every year since 2005. After growing a boutique brokerage in Marin, I purchased Pacific Union residential brokerage in 2009, which was branded and grown to the fifth largest residential brokerage in the country. In 2018, Compass bought the company for a record price. Out of two million actively licensed real estate agents in the United States, I'm currently ranked fifty-first in sales by the *Wall Street Journal*.[2] For the past ten years, I've been consistently ranked among the top seventy-five performers in the country. I thoroughly understand my craft. I love what I do. Yet every day I'm pleading with clients about the essential steps they need to take get the most value out of the purchase or sale of their home. Why?

*Trust.*

# ▎ TRUST IS EARNED

Buyers and sellers don't trust real estate agents. They hire someone to effectively manage what is likely their biggest asset, but they are reluctant to place their faith in what he or she says. An agent is the public face of real estate and exerts the biggest influence on the sale of a home, but it's not a face the public trusts. Buyers and sellers enter with a well-founded degree of skepticism.

Real estate agents don't command the same respect as other professionals because the educational, regulatory, and qualitative standards are abysmal. If you are having a midlife crisis and want to switch careers, go get your real estate license. If your husband traded you in for a younger model and you have to generate income, become a real estate agent. If you're a bored socialite and want to dabble, hang your shingle. Community college didn't work out? There's always real estate.

Residential real estate comprises roughly 30 percent of our nation's wealth.[3] The market collapsed in 2008–09 and the real estate industry has gone through extensive regulatory reform, yet the real estate sales community and their performance standards have remained relatively untouched.

The requirements to get a real estate license are less than rigorous. The time commitment sits somewhere between traffic school and getting an online minister's license; you must be eighteen years of age, complete 135 hours of education, get a background check, and pass an exam. No minimum hours of working experience or any sort of apprenticeship are required. All you need is a heartbeat, the right birth date, and less than four weeks of education, and you can get a license to represent buyers and sellers making what could be their biggest financial decision ever.

Real estate sales are essentially an investment advisory business, but it's not held to the same level of standards as, for example, the industry that sells and manages people's other primary asset class: securities. Most brokerage firms require that securities traders have a college education. Brokers must pass the Series 7 and Series 64 exams to buy and sell stocks, bonds, and mutual funds—and they must be sponsored by a legitimate brokerage firm to take the exams. On-the-job training prepares a broker to work with clients before taking on the responsibility of representing clients. If the real estate industry had more rigorous requirements for agents, buyers and sellers would likely be more inclined to accept the feedback they are given about their homes.

Real estate's low standards open the door for opportunistic agents who prey upon naïve, uninformed, or trusting clients. They don't last in the real estate business, but their behaviors undermine the public's trust. They say whatever serves their self-interest and are rarely held accountable. Their misrepresentations don't necessarily come in the form of bald-faced lies, but they just as effectively manipulate the truth—and their clients.

Unethical agents tell clients what they want to hear, rather than what they should hear, to get their business. *"Your house is an invaluable work of art and should be priced higher than any comp in the market."*

They pressure buyers into making offers by exaggerating competition. *"I hear two parties are going to be writing offers"* (though the house hasn't had any showings in six months).

They speak without knowing. *"I doubt that wall is load-bearing."*

They withhold essential information. *"It's a quiet family neighborhood"* (without mentioning that the street is a popular Waze detour during rush hour).

Though unscrupulous agents are in the minority, they cast a long shadow. They are why 67.5 percent of Americans polled in an online Google Consumer Survey do not trust real estate agents.[4]

# The Gatekeeper Is Gone

Technology is transforming the real estate business, and buyers and sellers are now awash in information, raising the question of whether they are equipped to represent themselves. Websites like Zillow, Trulia, Realtor.com, and Redfin empower consumers with data and knowledge about every corner of the real estate market. Survey findings show that 68 percent of Americans now start the home search on their own.[5] Buyers have apps that allow them to search for homes by street and neighborhood. They can drive around target areas and see what's for sale and the listing prices. Price history and tax information are readily available. Mortgage calculators are at their fingertips. Virtual tours take viewers inside homes. Online listings enable people to compare and contrast features of homes, winnowing down their search before they walk into a home. Home buyers and sellers are more educated about the market than ever before.

Technology's disruption creates much-needed transparency and efficiency in the real estate market, but there's a wide chasm between having information and expertise.

# I'm an Expert on the Dunning-Kruger Effect

Psychological research suggests that we are not great at evaluating ourselves accurately, and we frequently overestimate our own abilities. In 1999, two Cornell psychologists, David Dunning and Justin Kruger, coined the term "Dunning-Kruger effect" to describe a cognitive bias whereby people who are incompetent at something fail to recognize their own incompetence.[6] They don't know enough to realize what they don't know. Dunning's later research showed that people who have just a little bit of knowledge or success in a field tend to massively overestimate their abilities and get trapped in a "beginner's bubble" of inaccurate self-perception. Not only are they unable to see their incompetence, they're also likely to feel confident that they are competent.

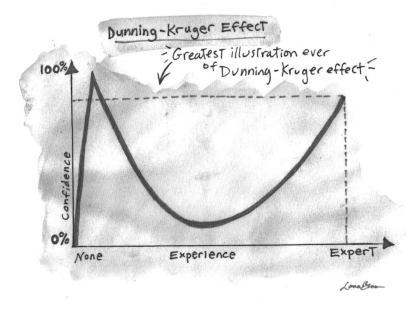

Perhaps no industry is more susceptible to the Dunning-Kruger Effect then residential real estate—and that further complicates the problem of agent credibility. People routinely overestimate their own real estate expertise when buying and selling a home. Homes are unusual assets because we live in them. We fall in love with homes in ways that we never do with our securities portfolio. Home is where we eat, sleep, raise children, open Christmas gifts, and celebrate Bar Mitzvahs, birthdays, and other rites of passage. It reflects our identity and tastes, and serves as a veritable memory bank. We think we know our homes inside and out, what they are worth, and how they would appeal to the marketplace. Homeownership, though, is different from the business of buying and selling homes. Most homeowners don't know enough about transacting homes to recognize their own lack of objectivity and expertise. A little knowledge can be a dangerous thing.

A soaring real estate market can further fuel people's delusions about their being real estate savvy. Homeowners fail to recognize that the rising real estate tide is often responsible for lifting all the boats, not their uncanny ability to time a market or create value in a home. Their passive success strengthens the belief that they are their own best guide in the real estate world—and they tune out their agent's counsel. Chances are, sellers who ride an up market are still leaving money on the table.

# **❙ THE BIND**

The story plays out over and over, regardless of the market or the real estate cycle. Buyers and sellers don't trust the expert—the person who traffics in the real estate market all day every day and understands its intricacies. So they grab the reins and direct the process themselves. Even though most people only enter the world of real estate once a decade, or perhaps once in a lifetime, many think they understand how it works. They are unaware of what they don't know, and they don't realize how emotions blind them to market realities.

Information about homes and markets only scratches the surface of what buyers and sellers need to maximize the value of their investment. The sophisticated and nuanced sales process often gets buried beneath the popular perception that one can hang a sign, post a listing on Redfin, negotiate a deal, and fill out the paperwork.

A wide range of overlapping skills is needed to successfully purchase or sell a home. You must be an expert at valuing properties. You must understand the psychology of pricing a home. You have to be attuned to the shifting design tastes of buyers and how the local demographic wants to live in their homes. Ideally, you are a concierge, possessing an ecosystem of stagers, designers, builders, and subcontractors who can quickly get a home ready for the market. Using your design acumen and resources, you show prospective buyers *how* to live in a home. You are skilled at marketing and branding, capable of building a story around a home that buyers remember. You have the negotiating skills to close a deal on favorable terms. Perhaps above all, you have to deliver the unvarnished truth, even if it includes messages that buyers and sellers don't want to hear.

## This Story Has a Happy Ending

I'm writing this book to show you the right way to buy and sell homes and set higher expectations for the professional services that your agent should deliver.

My goal is for this book to serve as the best guide ever to maximizing value on the purchase or sale of a home. In each chapter, I will explore one specific step in the home sale and acquisition process, explaining it in depth.

I don't recommend buying or selling property without expert representation, but if you are determined to be the captain of your own ship, this book will help you navigate the waters.

I have drawn on two aspects of my background in writing this book. First, my value-focused approach to real estate, which was shaped by buying and renovating residential homes. Before becoming an agent, my passion was finding homes that had fallen out of step with the market, reimagining what they could be, then renovating and selling them for a profit. I bought and sold over twenty homes in the western United States.

Each project served as a laboratory for understanding how to create spaces that people wanted to live in. I studied the entire process of home ownership—investing, renovating, and selling. I made a mistake on every single home, and took each lesson and rolled it into the next project. I invested my own money in each project. I learned to view houses, not just as homes, but as assets to monetize. And I carried that mindset into real estate after I became a licensed agent.

Second, I have worked for twenty years representing clients in the acquisition and sale of homes. I have witnessed how implementation of the principles laid out in this book has resulted in tremendous success for my clients.

This book provides a practical and disciplined approach to buying and selling a home. Along the way, I delve into the psychology of home buyers and sellers because investors' primary challenge is often themselves. The approach is simple, but it's not easy. Success in residential real estate is not about timing the market or outwitting the person on the other end of the negotiation—it's about adhering to a set of reasoned precepts that will guide you through each step of a process fraught with emotional and psychological traps. Follow this approach, and you will come out an absolute winner in the sale and purchase of your home.

# Chapter 1

# THERE ARE NO PICASSOS IN REAL ESTATE–VALUING A HOME

In 1990, a series of renowned experiments by Nobel Prize recipients Daniel Kahneman and Richard Thaler and coauthor Jack Knetsch revealed that we have an irrational tendency to overvalue something just because we own it, regardless of its objective value.[7] The researchers asked a large group to assign a value they would be willing to pay for a coffee mug. Half the participants were then given the mug for free and, soon after, the opportunity to trade their mug for an object of equal value. Classical economics assumes that people always behave rationally within an economic system and that the participants who were given mugs would maximize their welfare by trading for their preferred object. But it didn't work out that way. The owners of the mugs wanted, on average, twice the price they had been willing to pay for them. Simply owning the mug caused people to value it higher.

A later study showed that the value of a possession increases with the duration of ownership. The longer you own something, the more valuable it is, at least to you.[8]

The discovery that we value things more when we own them, a cognitive bias Thaler termed the "endowment effect," repeatedly shows up with homeownership. Regardless of the neighborhood or price tier, homeowners commonly believe the value of their home is higher than its actual market value. They think their home is that rare Picasso that defies market economics.

A paper published by the Reserve Bank of Australia revealed that about a quarter of homeowners think their property is worth up to 20 percent more than it is.[9] And the greater the owners' debt, the more they overestimate it. Hardly a seller in this country doesn't feel more qualified to render an opinion on value than the expert he or she hires. Unfortunately, living in a home doesn't make us experts in real estate.

Perception of value matters because the value of a house plays a role in many significant financial decisions. Home values shape household retirement plans.[10] Home values influence decisions on expenditures, with consumption going up by 5 to 7 percent of the perceived increase in housing wealth.[11] Above all, perceived home values dramatically impact the decision-making process when you elect to sell your home. Thinking your home is worth more than it is leads to overpricing, which can undermine the success of the sale.

How do homeowners shield themselves from the endowment effect—that stealthy, systematic error in thinking that impairs decision-making—when they are engaging in one of the biggest transactions of their life? Find an expert to value your home, an independent third party who has no emotional or financial connection to the property. Someone who does not view the home through the prism of the endowment effect.

The reality is that the value of your home is governed by comparable properties, likely right down the street from you. The residential real estate business is based on numbers, yet we often ignore the metrics and market data and make decisions based on what we want to believe. The value of a home has nothing to do with what we paid for it, or what we need to net from the sale, and this can be unwelcome information.

Part of the disconnect between homeowners and agents is that agents rarely break down their valuations in detail, engendering suspicion in clients. Clients conjecture that the valuation of their biggest asset is the product of a vague, faulty, or perhaps nonexistent process. In fact, arriving at a valuation is painstaking, arduous work, and it's one of the most important services an agent provides a client. The process and the building blocks should be transparent and described to clients in detail so that they can understand the valuation's underpinnings.

It's important to know what a home is worth, or can be worth, based on rational analytics, divorced from inflated ideas of value, wishful thinking, or false expectations created by others. Overpricing a home you are selling, or undervaluing a home you want to purchase, are costly mistakes.

In this chapter, I am going to deconstruct how homes are valued for purchase and sale, including the objective and subjective elements of the valuation. I'll also compare it with the other common method of assessing the value of a home—the lender's appraisal.

# THE MECHANICS OF HOME VALUATION

A comparative market analysis (CMA) is the standard valuation approach that a real estate agent undertakes. A CMA compares recently sold properties ("comps") that are similar to the subject property and adjusts for differences. Active listings are not used as comps because they only represent the seller's valuation and are not necessarily an indicator of market value.

To identify comps, agents can use sites like Redfin and Zillow, but the multiple listing service (MLS) has the most accurate and comprehensive information.

A CMA can determine market value only if the most comparable properties (i.e., the most similar) are selected. The key criteria for selecting the appropriate comps are timing, location, and property characteristics:

The date of sale should be as recent as possible. Sales more than a year old are less useful, particularly in fast-moving markets. The more recent the sales, the less likely the market has moved enough to render the comparable sale prices obsolete.

The comps should be in the same neighborhood, subdivision, or market—but be aware that there can be big disparities within a defined geographical area. Even being on the same street doesn't necessarily make the location of two properties comparable. One could be in a flat area, within a walking distance to town, while the other might be on a hill and require a car ride.

The comps should have as many of the property features of the subject home as possible, including the number of bedrooms and bathrooms, lot size, and age of the home. Ideally, the square footage of the comp should be within 15 percent of the subject home.

The agent then adjusts for the differences between the subject property and the comps. Comparing the fundamentals of properties—square footage, land, year built, number of bedrooms and bathrooms—for a CMA is a fairly objective and mechanical process. It's relatively easy to assign monetary value to, and then adjust for, the differences among these elements.

Websites like Zillow and Trulia capture millions of eyeballs every month using these variables as the basis for automated valuation models, but home buyers, sellers, and investors should be wary of using computer estimates to make decisions. It's like marrying someone based on a Bumble dating profile. Even Zillow acknowledges their estimates are inaccurate. Their chart of median error percentages in major cities runs between 4 and 7 percent.[12] Half of the home values in the area are closer than the error percentage and half are greater than the error percentage.

This is because, no matter how identical properties may appear, no two properties are exactly alike, and they differ in ways that are more complex to quantify. All factors that impact value must be evaluated. A diligent agent doing a CMA will add or subtract the amount that all material features contribute to or detract from the value of a comparison property.

# ❙ THE ART OF HOME VALUATION

Property valuation is an art, not a science. Appraisers and agents both build an opinion of market value based on data, but most would acknowledge that their methodology relies on gut instinct and experience. You can convince yourself you are scientific when valuing tract housing, but even when homes seem identical, judgments that impact pricing are necessary. This is especially true when it comes to a property's more subjective factors.

## Love Thy Neighbor…and Don't Block the View

I was once called to be an expert witness in a legal dispute between two homeowners in Belvedere, California. Belvedere is a small island off Tiburon with wraparound views of Sausalito, San Francisco, and the San Francisco Bay. The homeowners were neighbors who lived at opposite ends of a cul-de-sac facing the bay. The defendant had a forty-one-foot-high Acacia tree which blocked the plaintiff's view of one of the two towers of the Golden Gate Bridge. The plaintiff had never been able to see through that point in the property, but expansive views are worth millions of dollars in Belvedere, so it ended up in court. I was asked by the plaintiff to quantify the value of the obscured view of one tower of the Golden Gate Bridge.[13]

To value the view, I pulled the sales records of every property that traded on the view side of that street going back ten years. I examined historical photographs of each home to see whether it had a one-tower or a two-tower view. I compared the sale prices of similar homes with unobstructed views of both towers, those that could see only one tower, and those that had no view of the bridge. I accounted for other features that raised or lowered the value of each home as well. Then, I analyzed all the data and arrived at a valuation of $350,000 for the view, which was a little more than 1 percent of the original cost of building the bridge, not adjusting for inflation!

An accurate home valuation requires delving into the less tangible elements that enhance or lessen value in a home: the design and flow of the home, finishes, the outdoor living space, the contours of the land, curb appeal, and environmental factors, among others. The consideration and weighting of these factors is challenging, but makes all the difference in deriving the correct market value for a property.

Valuing these elements requires a deep understanding of the market, the neighborhood, the psychological factors that influence today's home buyers, and, above all, knowing what drives value in a home.

# What Buyers Want Drives Value

What buyers desire determines what the market "values." The more closely the characteristics of a home measure up to the desires of home buyers, the higher the value the home will be awarded in the marketplace.

Design and lifestyle trends—how people want to live in their homes—drive residential real estate values. It's a universal truth, whether you live in Topeka, New York, or London. People often think architects and designers are the arbiters of style, but it's buyers, and how they want to inhabit the spaces inside their homes, that propel design.

A shift in design taste happens every seven to ten years. As the seller, you must keep up with the shift if you don't want to leave money on the table. The following are the most important design and lifestyle trends to consider when valuing a home today.

## LIVING SPACE

The interior layout and design are critical factors in the valuation of a home. The overarching questions are, "How closely does the living space mirror what the current market wants? Does the layout reflect how buyers want to live in a home?"

Not all rooms are valued equally. The most highly valued rooms in today's market are an open kitchen connected to a family room, bedrooms, a secondary family room, and a home office for telecommuting. Extraneous spaces like a sauna, a walk-in wine cellar, a crafts room, or a massage room don't hold the same per-square-foot value. The price per square foot for these spaces gets adjusted down because they are not necessary for everyday living. For example, I valued a home in Sausalito, California, with an indoor pool. The owner thought it was a unique selling feature and wanted me to understand how special it was. He said, "How many homes in Marin have indoor pools?" as if its rarity made it more valuable.

I turned it back on him, "Right, how many homes in Marin have indoor pools?" followed by a long pause so my response could set in. "There's a reason. People don't value indoor pools—and the conditions they create with the steam and water—in an area that overlooks a bay with year-round gentle weather." Just because something is unique or rare, that doesn't make it valuable. The market must value it.

While there's no one-size-fits-all plan for living spaces, in the current market, the concept of an "open plan" living space has become the standard in home design. The days of compartmentalized rooms divided by doors and walls are gone, supplanted by a desire for open, connected living in a space that feels bigger.

The great room of this home in Belvedere, California, is an excellent expression of a beautifully designed open floor plan. Millennials, families, and empty nesters will all be attracted to the perfectly proportioned rectangular living space that accommodates informal dining at the kitchen island, more formal dining just off the kitchen, and a useful and relaxing living space adjacent to the fireplace. The scale of the furniture not only makes the room look larger, but also shows prospective buyers how they will live in the house. The message here is that spaces do not have to be big to be highly valued. The concept is applicable to most homes by creating a big, open great room, even if you have to remove a wall or two to do this.

Buyers want clear sight lines and a great room combining the kitchen, family room, and dining area, so they can interact with guests from the kitchen, watch the kids while they play, or have the whole family together, even if engaged in separate activities.

"Open plan" might spark images of grand, cavernous spaces, but the design is not limited to large homes. An apartment or cottage can combine multiple purposes in a tight space if the areas are clearly defined.

## CHECKLIST—LIVING SPACE

**Is the home's central living area a large, rectangular space with high ceilings? What is the scale of the home? Does the rest of the home have high ceilings, and do the spaces feel large and open?**

○ Is the floor plan optimal for everyday usage?

○ Is there a secondary family room to accommodate children as they grow older? How does the great room connect to the exterior living spaces?

○ In a family-driven market, is the master bedroom close to the children's bedrooms? Is the garage in close proximity to the kitchen?

○ Is there a mudroom between the kitchen and garage?

## FINISHES

Finishes are design elements that are usually attached to structural elements of a home, like walls, ceilings, and floors. Paint, flooring, appliances, countertops, and light fixtures are the dominant finishes in a home. The look and feel of the finishes can enhance or undermine market demand and desirability.

A home's finishes must align with what buyers desire. The level of finishes should also be commensurate with the pricing tier of the asset. A more expensive home will necessitate higher-end finishes. The brand and expense can be adjusted; it's the look and feel that's critical for resale.

Young buyers, in particular, place a premium on finishes. They want to walk into a space and feel like it's new. Accustomed to a fast-paced, always-plugged-in lifestyle, they have less downtime. Unlike previous generations, they are less likely to enter with a vision to remodel a home and a willingness to credit the seller for its positive attributes. They will severely discount an outdated home because all they can see is what you didn't do. They want to turn the key, unpack their suitcases, and get back on email.

---

## CHECKLIST–FINISHES

**A prudent seller will frequently flip through design magazines to be aware of what buyers and consumers want.**

○ Does the home have flooring consistent with contemporary demand? Do the kitchen and bathroom have contemporary countertops?

○ Do the bathroom fixtures look current?

○ Does the home have contemporary, chic lighting?

○ Does the kitchen have updated and matching hardware (hinges and doorknobs)? Does the home have matching stainless steel appliances?

○ Is the color palette of the carpet contemporary, and does it tie into the design of the home?

○ Does the home have a neutral wall color, or a color that's in demand?

---

## INDOOR-OUTDOOR LIVING

Indoor-outdoor spaces are in high demand and can add significant value to a property. Home buyers want a flowing design that erases the lines between the interior and exterior of the home. Almost every home aspires to connect with nature.

Gone are the days of simply having a table on the patio and throwing a few foldable chairs on the grass. The area formerly known as the "backyard" has evolved into another living space. People want to extend their homes into the outdoor spaces and bring more natural light inside, without the costs associated with expanding the square footage of their home.

If you are in a view-driven market, the highest valuation will be given to the "magical 1, 2, 3, 4 sequencing": a large, open great room that leads to a flat outdoor entertaining space that leads to a pool that leads to a view. The great room should have a focal point, a place your eyes are drawn to when you enter the space and, ideally, there should be a second focal point outside.

The principle of creating a visual point of interest off the main living space is not dependent on having a view or a pool. Whether you have a small terrace in an urban apartment or an expansive yard, having a focal point outside helps make a visual connection between the interior and exterior spaces. Highlight the best feature. Pick one point of interest in the outdoor living space on which to focus. It could be as simple as a tiny, vertical herb garden suspended from a wall, or a rectangular table with a bench and two chairs that push up against a balcony railing.

In the Home Trends Design Survey, the American Institute of Architects reported that requests for indoor-outdoor living increased for the sixth consecutive year in 2017. Seventy percent of the five hundred architecture firms sampled said there has been a rise in homeowners who want outdoor living space incorporated into the design of their homes.

The right landscaping on any property, whether an urban town home with a balcony and a greenbelt or a sprawling estate with rolling acres in the suburbs, impacts the valuation as well. According to a study by the University of Michigan, attractive landscaping increases a home's value by 5 to 7 percent.[14] The respondents to the study across seven states ranked sophistication as the most important element of landscaping—ideally a balance of large deciduous trees, evergreen plants, and hardscape.

Landscaping is an all-or-nothing game. You don't bandage Landscaping. If you put new elements amidst the old, the valuation gets discounted. A homeowner should either update the landscaping or leave it alone, but not muddle in between.

In most areas, a smaller, flat pad is valued higher than a larger, upslope property because families drive the market and they want an accessible, level area.

---

## CHECKLIST—INDOOR/OUTDOOR LIVING

○ Is there a level outdoor living space easily accessible from the great room or other public rooms in the house?

○ Do the outdoor living spaces have varied, defined experiences? Is there a lawn?

○ Is there enough hardscape for outdoor dining and entertaining? Is the hardscape in alignment with what today's buyers want? Is there a pool or spa?

○ Is the landscape design sophisticated? Does the property have mature vegetation?

○ Is the home well placed on the lot? Does the site placement maximize the backyard?

○ Which way is the home oriented, and does it get direct sun? Is the backyard private and quiet?

○ Is there a sport court?

---

## CURB APPEAL: AN INHERITANCE FROM OUR TRIBAL ANCESTORS

Curb appeal matters: houses that present well from the curb get higher valuations.

Humans are hardwired to react quickly to environmental cues—and it's difficult to change our impressions once formed. We make quick assessments in the first few seconds of our experience of someone or something. Research shows that our unconscious mind perceives in a few seconds what it takes our rational conscious mind much longer to evaluate and digest.[15]

Our snap judgments are an inheritance from our tribal ancestors who had to quickly determine if that rustling sound in the bush was a snapping twig or a saber-toothed tiger. Survival was dependent on the ability to make quick discernments. The proverbial tiger is gone and the brain has evolved, but the ancient part of the brain carries those caveman instincts into the modern world.

Although we are taught not to judge a book by its cover, we often do. And this certainly holds true in real estate.

Buyers' first impressions of homes are formed when they approach the curb or, more likely in the digital era, when they click on photos of a home online. According to a study by the Bank of Montreal[16], 80 percent of home buyers know if a house is right as soon as they walk in the door.

Dr. Michael Seiler, a professor of Real Estate and Finance at the College of William & Mary, led the first study using ocular tracking technology to record the exact eye scanning pattern employed by home buyers when searching the web for homes for sale.[17] He and his team created a typical home listing website, broken down into three sections. Overwhelmingly, participants (95.1 percent) first looked at the "curb appeal" photo—an enlarged photo that shows the exterior of the home. Then 76 percent of the viewers turned to the quantitative property description section, where details like the number of bedrooms, bathrooms, and square footage are displayed. Finally, the participants' eyes went to the real estate agent's remarks section, but 41.5 percent didn't even bother looking there at all. "Without an eye-catching photo, the battle is lost before it begins,"

Professor Seiler says. "You have to grab people's attention within two seconds. Do it the way a billboard does."

Curb appeal makes a statement about a house that hopefully lodges in the memory of the buyer. It's not about a grand façade or a rolling lawn. It's the details that thread together to leave a lasting impression. The right color paint for the exterior. A front door that grabs people's attention. Elegant door hardware, the first thing a buyer touches. Light fixtures that not only blaze a trail to your front door, but do it with style. Life and color with plants that frame the entryway and the walk up.

Vegetation that directs a buyer's attention to the best features of the façade. The hedge that screens off the Winnebago parked in the adjacent driveway. The fencing that defines the space and creates the impression of privacy. The wide-planked horizontal siding that masks the less attractive stucco.

---

## CHECKLIST–CURB APPEAL

○ Is the hardscape to the front door a material currently in demand? Is the landscape verdant and layered?

○ Does the home have the right color palette? Does it resonate with today's younger buyers?

○ Is the front door solid and its hardware appealing?

○ Does the doorway have a symmetrical composition of light fixtures and front door accents?

○ Does the vegetation accent the home's appeal?

○ Does the outside of the house look fresh, or weathered and peeling? Does the fence or gate define the property but not look foreboding? Is the driveway in good shape, or in disrepair?

---

> ○ Does the garage door accentuate the
> home's appearance?
>
> ○ Is there low-voltage landscape lighting to
> illuminate and frame the path? Does the mailbox
> complement the home?

## ENVIRONMENTAL FACTORS

Environmental factors don't show up in the MLS, but can dramatically impact the value of a home. A nearby cell tower, airport noise, overhead power lines, heavy traffic, or an interstate freeway that billows pollution are factors outside the boundaries of a property, and outside an owner's control, but they can play a role in devaluing a home. Rising water due to global warming is a concern for buyers in low-lying coastal areas. Negative environmental factors lower the valuation of a home.

Homeowners can mitigate some issues before the home is valued. The owner of a home with road noise could install a retaining wall with vegetation, or mount outdoor speakers and play music when the house is shown. If a house faces north and doesn't get direct sunlight, the seller can add LED lights and change the bulbs to brighten the inside. White crisp walls brighten a home if the natural lighting is not optimal.

## CHECKLIST—ENVIRONMENTAL FACTORS

○ Is there ambient road noise?

○ What is the microclimate in the area? What is the quality of the light?

○ What is the orientation of the house? Does it face west or south? Does it get direct sunlight?

○ Are there nearby cell towers? Are there overhead power lines? Does the home have privacy?

○ Is it located near a drug shelter or a homeless shelter?

○ Is there airport traffic? Is the home under a flight path? Are there issues with air or water quality?

○ Are there soil issues that would impact the cost and feasibility of use and future development?

## LOCATION

The two largest generations in America's history are dramatically shaping not just how, but where, people want to live. The baby boomers (born between 1946 and 1964 and numbering approximately seventy-seven million) and their millennial offspring (born from 1977 to 1996 and estimated around seventy-eight million) are waving goodbye to the car-centric McMansion era of oversized, ill-proportioned homes in favor of a more community-oriented lifestyle. As the boomers near retirement age, there's a trend to downsize and move into one-level homes in walkable, transit-friendly neighborhoods near suburban centers or mixed-use zones. Millennials tend to value efficiency and technology, and gravitate toward areas offering a mix of homes, stores, and other businesses within a short walk. In a National Association of Realtors research survey[18], the number of people who preferred a mixed-use suburban neighborhood was more than double the number who preferred a suburban neighborhood with houses only.

As suburban congestion increases, people place a greater premium on homes that have close proximity to freeways or public transport. In the San Francisco Bay Area, for example, commuters with a thirty-minute trip from home to work under congestion-free conditions spend 143 extra hours driving annually because of traffic.[19] What were once B-grade locations closer to the freeways to San Francisco now have greater cachet with buyers who want shorter commutes.

The era of living behind gates up long driveways has waned. There has been a return to village community living—valuing sidewalks, knowing one's neighbors, and dropping the hedges.

---

### CHECKLIST–LOCATION

○ Is the home in the flats or in the hills?

○ Is it walking distance to town?

○ If a suburban home, does it have access to freeways? Does it have a "village" lifestyle?

○ Is it walkable to goods and services (school, town, shopping)? Does it have easy access to bus or metro lines?

○ Does it feel secure and protected?

---

# AN APPRAISAL OF THE APPRAISAL

While an agent performs a CMA, a lender's professional appraiser will perform their own appraisal, an unbiased opinion, of a home's value. Unfortunately, they don't always yield the same results, and this can be frustrating. Why the discrepancy?

The differences are largely driven by who's doing the evaluation and its purpose. Agents produce CMAs for their clients to assess the purchase or sale price. A lender's agent, by contrast, performs an appraisal on behalf of the bank to verify that the lender is not making a loan for more than the home is worth. In theory, the appraiser is supposed to be protecting not only the bank, but also the foolish buyer who is willing to pay too much for the property.

An appraiser has no financial ties to the transaction and delivers a defensible and carefully documented opinion of value devoid of bias. A commissioned agent, by contrast, is a stakeholder in the transaction.

Home buyers want high appraised values so they can get a mortgage. Mortgage lenders want conservative values so that their loan is less risky. Appraisers are caught in the middle.

Historically, lenders and agents were directly involved in picking appraisers, but in the wake of the 2008 housing crisis, Fannie Mae and Freddie Mac instituted the Home Valuation Code of Conduct to prohibit handpicking appraisers.[20] The Code was designed to make it difficult for lenders to pressure appraisers into dishing up the "right" value. A bank must now use an appraisal management company to pluck an appraiser from its pool.

Appraisers are given a copy of the home purchase contract, so they know the purchase price. This may seem odd, but the appraisal is done to support a specific purchase price, and not to generate an independent purchase price. That's why many appraisals will often substantiate the agreed price. Doesn't this mean the appraiser's opinion of fair market value is necessarily influenced by the purchase price? It does not. The idea is that appraisers are uninterested parties selected at random—they earn no benefit for rendering a particular valuation.

Agents' and appraisers' valuation methodologies overlap—both are influenced by recent sales of similar properties and current market trends. An appraiser, however, is held to more rigorous standards. An appraiser must determine that the theoretical buyer or seller is "well-informed," and can make decisions without "undue stress" and engage in an "arm's-length" transaction.

Just because a home sells at a particular price, that doesn't mean that's its market value. If a parent sells a home to a child at a discount, that doesn't become the new price benchmark in that neighborhood. Conversely, when a property is bid up with multiple offers, that price doesn't necessarily reflect market value by appraisers' standards.

A property in San Francisco's frenzied real estate market had nineteen purchase offers. The appraiser, however, rendered a valuation much lower than the purchase price because the comps didn't support the sales price. The buyer was angry with the appraiser: "What do you mean you can't support the price? How can you say it's not worth that price if eighteen other people are willing to pay what I'm paying?" The appraiser responded, "If all it took were a ratified contract to validate the worth of a property, banks wouldn't need to have an appraisal done. In a market where there's a feeding frenzy, things get bid up above what can be supported by the best comps. No closed sales support this price."

To some degree, appraisers are always chasing the market with historical data.

I've had many situations where I've said to clients, "This home may not appraise out. I'm not saying you are paying too much. It's just about the comps. So be prepared." Most of the time in higher-end markets, the buyer is willing to put more money down to reduce the loan-to-value (LTV) ratio to close the sale.

# Does a Valuation or an Appraisal Better Reflect the Market Value of a Home?

Agents' and appraisers' valuations serve different functions. The question of which better reflects the market value of a property ultimately depends on the definition of "market value." If market value means the most probable price that a property should be worth in a competitive market where there is no undue stress to buyers or sellers, an appraisal is a better tool.[21] If your definition of market value is the price a home would sell for in the current market, an agent's valuation is more relevant and timely.

Appraisals are supposed to mimic the market, but their valuations often lag the market, particularly when it's moving quickly. If inventory is thin and prices are soaring, finding accurate and timely valuations that support sales is challenging—and lenders don't want to risk funding or selling a loan without a supporting valuation.

Agents know more about current value than appraisers because they are intimately familiar with properties in their market. Agents know the history and story of each property. They know other agents and the dirt about what's going on. Agents cover a limited geographical area, whereas appraisers cover a wider territory and don't possess the same exhaustive local knowledge. For these reasons, appraisers rely on input from agents. I routinely receive calls from appraisers about properties in my community, even about homes I'm not representing, because they know I have valuable information that can't be found on the MLS or gained from a brief visit to the property.

Chapter 2

# THE PRICE BETTER
# BE RIGHT

I once represented the seller of a home in Mill Valley, a charming town just across the Golden Gate Bridge from San Francisco. After making extensive constructive improvements to the home, I showed the sellers the numbers on the most recent home sales in their community. I also brought in five colleagues to provide their objective opinions of value. The comps, the other agents, and my own valuation all pointed to a market value between $3.5 and $3.6 million. As I reviewed the data with Linda, the owner, I could sense an immediate resistance to the suggested list price. When I concluded my presentation, Linda didn't comment on any of the numbers we had painstakingly assembled. She responded, "I think my home is worth $3.8 million," and provided her rationale.

Linda's valuation was a product of her original purchase price, the money she had invested in the house, the length of time she had owned it, the sale price of a couple of her friends' homes in an adjacent neighborhood, and a reading from her astrologer who said she saw a three and an eight in the home's value.

Remember, this is California.

Linda left the meeting tight-lipped and went dark for three days. We couldn't launch the listing on the MLS as scheduled. My hands were tied, and we were up against the clock for the scheduled broker's open. Finally, Linda returned my call, and I said, "You have to trust me. I've been doing this for a long time, and I have nothing but your best interests at heart. We just spent three months making constructive improvements to sell your home for the highest price. You're going to shoot yourself in the foot if you over-price your home. You want $3.8 million. If you list at that price, it will sell between 3.4 and $3.5 million because of the perception that it's overpriced."

Linda reluctantly agreed to put it on the market at $3,595,000. Several buyers emerged. An agent called and reported that his client could only afford the list price, and they knew it would go over asking. He asked, "Should my client still make an offer?" "Absolutely," I advised. "You never know what's going to happen. Please have them write the offer." In real estate, you want offers from the people who can only afford the listing price to drive interest from the people who can pay more for the house. When a more qualified buyer who can afford more knows someone else is in play, that buyer will often pay more. Competitive bidding pushed the price up and the house sold for $4.2 million. By following my advice and strategic pricing, Linda made $400,000 over what she originally wanted for the house!

So how do you arrive at the magic number to price a home? For every home I sell, I undertake the same price-setting process. I complete the comparative market analysis (CMA). Then, I bring in four to seven colleagues to give me their opinion on a home's value. Finally, I meet with the seller to set the listing price. I present the market data, the opinions of my colleagues, and my own opinion about the listing price of the house. I then ask for the seller's perspective. Sellers, like Linda, generally have higher numbers in mind. They ask, "How do I know I won't be underpricing the house?"

The pricing strategy for a home dramatically impacts the financial success of the transaction. Agents will give different advice about the appropriate pricing tactic. Many will tell you that a higher-than-market price begets a higher-than-market sale price; in the worst case, the real estate crosswinds will blow you back to market value. Others recommend listing the home under market value with a view toward attracting more offers, to drive the sale price over asking, and possibly well above market value.

The answer is that setting the price in the middle or lower end of the range of a home's value generates the biggest return for the seller in any market. The market always drives a home to its absolute highest value in the short term if the property is priced at or below market value. But the housing market is not nearly as kind if a home is overpriced. The market doesn't necessarily take the asking price down to real market value. It often pushes the home well below its real value, for practical and psychological reasons.

I used to think the market was efficient on the upside but inefficient if overpriced, but that's not the case. Real estate economist Selma Hepp points out, "The market is actually overcorrecting in both instances. The market adjusts beyond what's usual, beyond market value."

Let's examine the psychology underpinning these dynamics.

# ▌ GOING, GOING, GONE

In real estate, you will never be in a better position than waking up with two or more offers waiting in your inbox. The pressure of competition is what drives buyers to pay more than market value for a home, enabling sellers to get a sale price that would not have been possible had the home originally been listed at that price point. Unless buyers experience the pressure of another bidder, they will take their time and act rationally.

When selling a home, I create a pricing structure that makes prospective buyers feel like they are going to lose it if they don't act immediately. A perceived lower starting price energizes buyers to engage—and when there's a crowded field, buyers' behavior becomes less rational. With the pressure of just one more bid, buyers of a home quickly find themselves willing to overpay in order to win the home away from the others.

Renowned behavioral economist Dan Ariely of Duke University has demonstrated that lower starting prices in auctions lead to higher-than-expected final prices. He studied eBay online auction behaviors and noted that when sellers lowered prices, sometimes below the opportunity cost of the items offered, more bidders entered the process. The sellers set low opening prices to attract low-value bidders who in turn attracted high-value bidders.[22] Even though other auctions may offer similar products, buyers demonstrate bias for auctions with more bids. Buyers are more comfortable—and emboldened—when others are vying for the same product.

"Herding" is a psychological concept about people who make decisions as part of a group that they would not make individually. Operating under the "three heads are better than one" maxim, individuals find it hard to believe that a large group could be wrong. Humans are influenced by group behavior, believing the group knows something they don't. They jump on the bandwagon, and it turns into a bidding war.

Ariely refutes the idea that we always act in fundamentally rational ways. We overpay for an auction or pay more than "market value" for a home, but these behaviors, while not rational, are not random or senseless. They are predictable, systematic—and very human, or, as he captures in the title of his book, *Predictably Irrational*.

The evidence for my pricing strategy is obviously anecdotal, but I have twenty years of anecdotes that support the thesis—and hundreds of colleagues echo the sentiment. The skeptics might say agents have ulterior motives. Agents want to close the transaction as quickly as possible, and a lower pricing strategy serves that end. But there's no way an agent could build a successful business over a long period of time by underselling homes. An agent works in a relatively enclosed community and relies completely on the feedback and referrals of clients.

## Don't Let Your Home Be a High-Priced Bread Maker

Pricing a home above market value under the theory that "everyone likes to negotiate" is failed logic. Overpricing and negotiating may be an effective strategy to sell knock-off sunglasses in an outdoor market in Bangkok, but overpricing a home stops buyers in their tracks. Sellers who believe buyers will just appear and make their best offer do not understand how the market functions. It's challenging to get buyers shopping online to even enter a home. If a home is priced 5 percent or more above comparative listings, the number of buyers who tour the home drops precipitously. Those who do visit will be inclined to negatively compare the home with better-priced homes.

Agents will effectively use your overpriced home to sell other homes. When one home looks overpriced, a buyer might be inclined to purchase another property that wasn't initially in his or her crosshairs because the overpriced home makes it appear a good value by comparison. You are selling other listings by overpricing your home.

Marketing experts often employ this tactic. In the 1990s, Williams-Sonoma brought a bread maker machine to the market for the first time, and put a $275 price tag on it. Sales were sluggish, so they did something seemingly counterintuitive. They brought another "deluxe" bread maker to the market that was virtually identical and priced it almost 50 percent higher. Sales skyrocketed—of the original bread maker.

Consumers had a basis of comparison and the lower-priced product suddenly looked much more attractive.

The lesson: don't let your home be used as a stalking horse by overpricing it.

## Why Don't They Just Make an Offer?

Sellers who aren't receiving offers on overpriced homes often think, "Buyers can just make an offer, can't they?" The answer is yes. But serious buyers will often not make an offer on an overpriced home for a variety of psychological reasons.

Negotiating with an unmotivated seller is demoralizing.

Buyers will think the owner is so unrealistic that it's not worth their time to make an offer. Home buyers are busy and don't want to engage an unmotivated seller.

They won't want to insult the owner, concerned they are going to burn a bridge for future negotiations if they present a "lowball" offer, even though it's not a lowball offer.

# ▍THE GOLDEN DAYS

The first seven to ten days after the release of the listing is the most critical period. There's a limited pool of buyers who are eagerly waiting for your home to come on the market. You have one opportunity to capture that limited buying pool. If you don't get it right, you can never recapture the momentum and the pent-up demand of those buyers. If the price or the way the house presents doesn't resonate with buyers, they move on to the next week's listing. The market is highly punitive to homes that are overpriced or not presented well. You are now in a position of defense, rather than offense, because all the existing buyers have moved on. Instead of being in control and having buyers line up outside your front door, you are defending the price and chasing every new buyer who comes into the marketplace.

The new buyers are not driven by emotion. The urgency is gone. They have a more jaundiced view, wondering if something is wrong with the home. A home that sits idle on the market can blemish an entire neighborhood. Buyers can start to wonder, "What's wrong with the area?"

You cannot recapture the excitement and enthusiasm that accompanies bringing a property to market unless you make a significant price drop. The price drop is generally well below what the market's initial perception of value would have been.

Zillow tracked homes listed over the course of a year to better understand the relationship between the number of days on the market and the final sales price.[23] Across the United States, Zillow found that homes that were on the market for a week traded almost at the listing price. Homes that were on the market for 80 days ended up with a median sales price 6 percent below listing price. Homes on the market for 169 days had a median sales price 9 percent below listing price.

# PRICE REDUCTIONS—DON'T BURN THE CLOCK

If you insist on listing at a high price, gauge the response carefully and get the price down immediately if it's tepid.

Small price reductions are a waste of time. Sellers might hope they can close just below their original price, but these discounts do little to motivate buyers—and they burn the clock. Incremental price drops only communicate to the marketplace, "I'm still an unrealistic seller. I still don't get it. I'm still not willing to sell my house for what it's worth."

If a home has been stigmatized by being overpriced, all is not lost. Sellers can inject life into a moribund listing by acting quickly, but they must make a dramatic price adjustment of 8 to 10 percent or more to effect any real change. The typical reaction of sellers: "Buyers will think we are desperate." I say, "To the contrary, you are telling the market that you are now a realistic seller." It's not shameful to make a price reduction if you made a mistake at the outset. It's the only way to grab the attention of previous buyers who dismissed the home, but equally important, the adjustment allows the home to drop down to a new tier of buyers. Without the reduction, the home is not reaching that level of buyers.

When a home is overpriced, you only hear about what's wrong with it. When a price gets adjusted or corrected, especially quickly, all you hear about is what's great about the house. The prospective buyer criticism evaporates and the glass that was half empty turns half full.

# ▎THE ANCHOR BIAS

Those who advocate more aggressive pricing for homes believe that a higher price tag will connote greater value in buyers' minds. Anchoring is a cognitive bias identified by Nobel-Prize-winning psychologist Daniel Kahneman and his partner, Amos Tversky.[24] They discovered that humans are irrationally influenced by the first piece of information (the anchor) presented to them when making decisions. In home buying, the theory is that the first number we see colors any number that follows. When home buyers hear an initial price (the anchor), they unconsciously give disproportionate weight to that number (the bias) and adjust from that starting point. The concern is that a property priced "low" may command a lower sale price because buyers become unconsciously "anchored" to the initial low perception of value. The theory, therefore, is that sellers should err on the high side when pricing homes to produce a higher final sales price.[25]

The anchoring bias may exist under certain market conditions, but my overwhelming experience is that an overpriced home will sit on the market, and there's a strong probability that it will ultimately trade below market value. An accurately priced home will sell. An underpriced home will get driven up to its market value and perhaps above it.

## Dollars and Sense

I always use a "just below" or "charm" pricing strategy with homes, putting a 95 in the listing price, rather than a "century" (round) number. For example, I list a home at $295,000 or $2,495,000. The approach is both practical and psychological.

If a price stays under a large number threshold, it's going to be discovered by more computer searches. According to a report by the National Association of Realtors, 90 percent of buyers search online during the home buying process.[26] Most buyers search within a target price range that they can afford. The fractionally less expensive home that's under, rather than at, the upper pricing tier is going to appear in more search results.

The more important advantage is psychological. Our brains *perceive* the price to be lower. Everyone has the mental ability to round up from $2,495,000 to $2.5 million and recognize that the prices are essentially the same—so why price just below? The answer is heuristics. The brain is constantly computing and looking for the most efficient way to consolidate the vast amount of information that floods in. Heuristics are hardwired mental shortcuts that the human brain uses to make judgments and routine decisions. We read from left to right. According to research, the brain works so quickly that before even before it finishes reading a multi-digit number, it has unconsciously begun to store the leftmost digits. That's what we remember.

Rounding down to the next significant monetary unit makes a psychological impact. There's a reason the 99 Cents Only Stores aren't the "$1.00 Only Stores." It wasn't a coincidence that Steve Jobs's 99 cents per song iTunes strategy saved the music industry from file sharing and free downloading. People feel they are getting greater value.

Michael J. Seiler, a real estate professor at the College of William & Mary and the coauthor of a study on home pricing strategies, found that "the just-below pricing strategy yields the highest transaction price relative to the true underlying home value."[27] On average, the houses whose sellers employed the strategy averaged about a 2 percent higher return, a significant amount when homes are worth hundreds of thousands or millions of dollars.

Home purchases are emotional decisions. Small factors that influence a buyer to feel more comfortable paying a price do make a difference.

# WINTER, SPRING, SUMMER, OR FALL: WHEN TO SELL YOUR HOME

When I got started in the business, spring selling season meant when the daffodils were coming out of the ground during April, May, and June. In Marin, that's when homes traditionally went on the market. The prevailing wisdom was that most families want to move when the kids are out of school.

People would buy houses at a ferocious pace until the second or third week of May. Then they'd go on to graduations and travel for the summer. There'd be a window in the fall to sell homes, and then you'd hit November and Christmas and those six weeks were wiped out. By the second or third week of January, people would start thinking, "I want to be in a new house by the time my kids start school in September. I better start looking now."

I thought, "What am I doing? There are no houses on the market in January. It's always about supply and demand in business. The oversupply of homes is what kills business. Why don't I list homes during the second or third week of January when there's no competing inventory?" Twelve or thirteen years ago, I started listing homes in January and others followed. The selling season is now greatly expanded in Marin.

A study by the online brokerage Redfin[28] affirms that the principle holds true across the country. They found that the average seller nets more above asking price during the months of December, January, February, and March than from June through November, even in cold-weather places like Chicago and Boston. According to the study, homes listed in winter also sell faster than those posted in spring.

Chapter 3

# PREPARING A HOME FOR SALE

After watching sellers leave money on the table by failing to update their homes before putting them on the market, I decided to make pre-listing improvements to homes the nucleus of my efforts for seller representation. I hands-on update, renovate, and stage approximately 85 percent of the homes that I list and sell. While it takes far more time and effort on my end, I liken it to playing offense rather than defense. Instead of reacting to sellers' predictable critiques about out-of-style finishes or easily addressable structural or design issues, I proactively improve a home. I understand the design demands of buyers and I bring the homes I'm selling into alignment with those demands.

Agents are paid a lot for what they do, and the days of passively putting a "For Sale" sign in the ground and printing a few marketing brochures should be long behind us. Properly preparing a home for the market is one of the keys to getting the highest possible return on your investment.

## THE TIMES THEY ARE A-CHANGIN'

Buyers only pay a premium for what's in style. The closer the palette, the finishes, and the layout are to what buyers want, the more money a seller makes. The design world of homes changes in the blink of an eye and, if you are like most homeowners, you probably don't realize it. Floor-to-ceiling wood paneling, once considered a rich and natural look, now makes a space dark and unappealing in a culture that values light. Formal living spaces, the definition of luxury in decades past, have been replaced by the comfort and functionality of casual living. Shiny brass bathroom fixtures were all the rage when Gordon Gecko roamed Wall Street, but now they instantly date a home.

A homeowner must stay updated on design trends to understand what the market wants. We are fortunate to be living in an era when design education is at our fingertips. Twenty years ago, people waited for the next edition of *Architectural Digest* to come out to understand what their homes should look like. Now homeowners have multiple options to follow design trends.

It's as easy as picking up a design magazine or clicking on a handful of leading websites. My favorites are *Dwell, Elle Decor,* Houzz.com, Pinterest, and Apartment Therapy.com. Then there are the new kids on the block: the hundreds of bloggers who capture and direct design styles. Bloggers are the voice of the people. They don't have a large staff, and they lean toward the practical application of design and style.

Study those images and implement what people want in terms of palette, textures, layout, and even spatial planning for furniture placement when you update your home.

Home design, though, is not just visual; it's experiential. Ideally, homeowners can touch furniture and textiles and feel the ambience created by great interior design. To that end, one home design retailer stands above the rest in creating an inspiring and immersive physical environment—Restoration Hardware, or RH, as they've been rebranded. The company offers stunning design spaces where homeowners can get a better feel for what the market wants, experiences we don't often have unless we're staying at an upscale hotel or visiting a friend's home that's tastefully done.

In the wake of the implosion of the financial markets in 2008–09, and in the face of retailers scrambling to move their businesses online, Restoration Hardware CEO Gary Friedman responded with a counterintuitive strategy: he doubled down on brick-and-mortar spaces. The company invested millions of dollars building inspiring "galleries" in place of traditional stores. Stores or showrooms typically focus on items or categories. Friedman's idea was to create a destination for people to experience great design. He wanted to break down the walls between the retail and residential worlds and create aspirational, multifaceted spaces, awash in natural light, that leave visitors with the feeling "I want to live here. I want my home to feel like this."

The company has successfully tapped into American culture's affinity for modern products and homes. Both millennials and their baby-boomer parents embrace modernism, albeit for different reasons. Millennials, who are quickly becoming the generation that drives the real estate market, grew up with a minimalist modern aesthetic, reflected in their embrace of all things Apple and their tech-dominated work environments. The baby boomers weren't surrounded by the trappings of technology, but value modernity because of their emphasis on youth and well-being. The confluence of the two generations and Friedman's vision has turned the iconic brand into a verb. I regularly hear buyers make comments like, "We can 'Resto' the house and make it current so buyers pay up for it!"

Updating and staging a home are essential if you want to maximize the return on your investment. Making certain strategic changes to a house before it goes on the market will elevate it into a higher pricing tier. These are relatively quick amendments that signal to buyers that they can simply turn the key. Very few homes—maybe one or two out of every thirty homes sold—don't need anything more than a stylist showing up to push around the existing furniture and edit out personal contents.

Pre-listing constructive improvements will not only sell a home more quickly, but also provide a three to four times return on the dollars spent. Staging is even more critical—and the wrong place to try to save money. If there is a three to four times return on capital improvements, staging provides a ten to fifteen times return.

The exception to this rule is a home that has pervasive structural issues. At a certain point, deferred maintenance can relegate a house to "lot value," meaning no value is assigned to the structure. If your home falls into this category, leave it alone and sell it for lot value, unless you have the money to completely rebuild it.

# ▋ HOME SWEET HOME

*"But my home is beautiful."*

*"People love coming into our home."*

*"My home was designed by [well-known interior designer]."*

*"We are not doing one thing to this house."*

Defending one's home is a kneejerk response I get from 90 percent of my clients. People love their homes. They are conditioned to living in their homes in a particular manner. They cannot see beyond chandeliers, a color palette, or wallpaper from twenty years ago. They were enraptured with those styles when they chose them, and the feeling never faded.

We fall in love with our homes like we fall in love with the music of our youth.[29] My head aches if I listen to a pop station today, but throw on George Michael's 1990s track "Freedom" and I feel happy. No matter how sophisticated my musical tastes have grown in the intervening years, my brain is stuck on the songs that evoke memories and feelings from an earlier period of life. Our homes hold a similar power over our emotions—and that can be a problem when it comes time to sell.

If, and when, you are ready to emotionally disconnect from your home, and can look at it as an asset and no longer the place where you raised your children and celebrated special occasions, you will be in a position to maximize its value.

I had a listing in Ross, California, a community that trades to bankers, tech start-up executives, and film industry people. It was a beautifully designed home, but had dark, exotic wood throughout the kitchen, bathrooms, library, and across the ceilings. Women, who often drive the home search process, have a visceral distaste for interior wood. Wood is very masculine, evoking images of ships and cigar rooms, and is a difficult sell in upscale markets. I begged the seller, who had already moved out, to paint out the cabinets. He was vehement in his objection: "This wood is no longer available on the marketplace and was an integral part of the original design. You can never go back once you paint wood. I won't do that." I responded, "Why would you want to roll the clock back to the turn of the century? If you have a passion for architectural preservation, you are better off donating to the local historical society. And if you have already moved and you are never returning to the home, why do you care?" But people do care because, emotionally, they haven't let go. They are still hearing the George Michael soundtrack.

Every time a buyer came to see the house, I heard the same comments: "I almost didn't come when I saw dark wood throughout the house." I sold the house four months after it went on the market. It would have sold far quicker had I been able to resolve that issue. Keeping the cabinets in natural wood cost the sellers an additional four months in mortgage payments/carrying costs and likely reduced the overall sale price by 5 percent.

If you really care about making money on your home, divorce yourself from emotional attachments. Your preferences and memories are irrelevant to your prospective purchaser pool. It's time for the next owner!

## FEELING MISUNDERSTOOD AND DEPRECIATED

A buyer named Mark engaged me to represent his home after having no luck selling it with another agent. He purchased the home at the peak of the market in 2007. In the intervening years, Mark had not done anything to it, apart from basic upkeep. The home was ten years more dated than it had been when he purchased it. Mark's frustration was palpable. "Tracy, we think we overpaid for the house when we bought it. It's not worth any more than we paid for it. We listed it slightly higher than our purchase price, and crickets. We had no offers." I said, "You paid fair market value for it in an inflated market. You didn't make any capital improvements to the home. Your house depreciated every year. The market went up. Your house went down. And your investment flatlined."

Homeowners often think that a house is an appreciating asset, whereas the physical structure actually depreciates. Toilets, roofs, plumbing, windows, doors, floors, and electrical systems degrade over time. Much as a new car falls in value as soon as you drive it off the lot, time exacts a toll on every home from the moment it's occupied. That's why the government allows homeowners to take a tax deduction for the depreciation of the structure.

That raises the question Mark then asked: "If houses are depreciating assets and expensive to maintain, why are people making so much money on homes while mine has seemingly flatlined?"

Real estate prices are governed by the law of supply and demand. In the simplest terms, when there's high demand for homes in an area with a limited supply of properties, prices rise. Many factors impact supply and demand. Lower interest rates translate to less expensive mortgages and strengthen demand. Economic growth leads to greater income, giving people more money to spend on homes.

Low unemployment heightens demand. Relaxed lending standards in mortgage markets bring more buyers to the table. Strong consumer confidence emboldens people to make the leap into home ownership. And the inverse of each of these factors is also true, leading to falling home values.

These macroeconomic dynamics, to varying degrees, influenced the value of Mark's home ten years after he purchased it, but they equally affected the comparable homes whose values had risen. Two predominant factors explain the perceived stagnation of Mark's home's value vis-à-vis the others: the timing of the original sale and the condition of the home. Why are these so significant?

# A BROKEN CLOCK IS RIGHT TWICE A DAY: TIMING THE MARKET

Mark bought his home at the peak of the housing market in 2007, just ahead of the catastrophic market collapse. From 2008–11, housing prices fell by 27 percent in Marin County.[30] From 2012–17, the market rose by approximately 55 percent.[31] Homes appreciated over the course of those ten years by a net 28 percent. Those neighbors who were "making so much money on homes" that Mark referenced likely had a different buy-in point. Should Mark be faulted for not timing the market?

Trying to time a real estate market is a fool's errand. Buying or selling a home based on the prediction of future market value is a strategy that has left many investors on the sidelines for years at a time during market run-ups. One must also weigh the strategy against the unique sense of material happiness that comes with owning a home. Several factors complicate attempting to time the market.

The majority of buyers and sellers are owner-occupiers. Their decision to buy a home is driven by events like marriage, a baby, or a job change. They don't have the luxury of trying to time the market.

The length and unpredictability of housing market cycles make it very difficult to time the market. Housing cycles typically go through four phases: expansion, oversupply, recession, and recovery. Buyers got lucky if they bought in 2010 when prices bottomed out, but those who decided to wait until the market dropped further would have waited eight additional years because the United States economy has enjoyed its second-longest expansion in history (at the time of writing). Every market cycle is a different length of time. It's hard to tell when the price turning point will come. And a housing market may not turn at all if that market is undersupplied.

Barriers to homeowner mobility undermine an investor's ability to time the market. Sellers may profit by selling a home, but they usually need to move into another home in the same market where prices have risen, unless they are moving out of the area. People can also feel locked into their homes because they have low mortgage rates and they are reluctant to give up the loan when they sell. Economists call the phenomenon the "lock-in effect."[32]

Trying to perfectly time the market is extremely difficult, even for professional investors. Market timers have to get it right twice: when they enter and when they exit the real estate market. Many personal and family factors come into play when purchasing a home, beyond potential financial gain, that complicate one's ability to time the market.

The answer is no—we can't fault Mark for failing to time the market.

# ▌ CONDITION OF THE HOME

However, the condition of Mark's home, the second and more important factor underlying the lack of appreciation of Mark's home's value, was in Mark's exclusive control. Mark did not update the home to meet the demands of the current market. He was selling a rotary dial phone in the digital age.

Any world-class performer—whether an athlete, businessman, or artist—knows that a key to success is differentiating what is and what is not within your control. The more attention you devote to those things you can control, the greater the impact on ultimate performance. Mark was solely in charge of the condition of his home, and he chose not to dedicate any capital toward counteracting the inevitable obsolescence of the physical structure.

Improving a home while living in it can seem expensive and disruptive for many homeowners. The enormity of the task may seem greater at the time of sale, and feel like an extra and unnecessary expense. Some homeowners, like Mark, are simply surprised that they need to do anything at all to their homes. They move in, get comfy, and stop paying attention to home design trends, if they ever did. It's analogous to being married for a long time. After a while, you stop trying to impress your spouse with your fashion savvy. You show up at the dinner table wearing your threadbare college sweatshirt, sweatpants, and flip-flops. You value comfort over style. You care less about the external presentation because your spouse gets who you are. He or she sees you. Your outfit isn't an impediment to that person's experience of you. But selling a house is like reentering the dating world. People don't know you and will swipe left if you are sporting feathered bangs or that Members Only jacket.

I agreed to represent the property on the provision that Mark would update it. My team came in; we renovated the home, put it on the market, and finally sold it for a profit.

# | KNOW THY MARKET

In preparing a home for the market, a seller needs to understand the design demands of the market, how people want to live in their homes, and what commands top dollar. A good agent should educate sellers on market demands and spearhead the process of updating and staging a home.

If there is no design-savvy agent to orchestrate the renovation process, a home stager or interior designer can take on the role. The caveat is that they are not experts in home valuation. Neither necessarily understands what moves homes at different pricing tiers in different communities. And their names are not on the line with respect to how the home is going to trade.

Let me illustrate what happens when you renovate or build without knowing what the market desires. A first-time developer raised money from a small group of investors and bought a home with a beautiful flat pad and extensive views of San Francisco Bay. The sale of her house should have been a home run, but she never consulted with anyone who really understood the supply-and-demand dynamics and the desires of local buyers. Instead, she hired an architect to do the renovations. Architects don't consult on the market. They design and build in accordance with the desires of their clients. Architects are not thinking about resale value when they are designing.

The owner colossally overpriced the four-thousand-square-foot home at $7.3 million. She walked into my office in tears three months after it went on the market. "You have to help us," she pleaded. "We hired the wrong person. We should've called you in the beginning." She wanted to fire their agent. I said, "Don't do that. She didn't do anything wrong. You designed and priced the home. I will help out, but you're not going to get rid of your agent." I liked her agent. She was very capable.

The architect had designed a family home that was sexy from the outside, but he left critical pieces for buyers out of the floor plan. There was only one bathroom for three children's bedrooms. The backyard was plumbed for a pool, but a pool wasn't built. The old garage floor remained in what was essentially a new home. The kitchen was too small for the size of the home.

If the owner had understood that she was selling her home in a family-driven market that demands a family floor plan, she would have added en-suite bathrooms next to the kids' bedrooms. She would have built a secondary playroom because buyers want to know the kids are going to have their own space away from the parents when they are teenagers. Instead of a walk-in wine cellar, she would have designed a larger kitchen. And she would have built a pool, rather than just plumbing for a pool and passing the buck to her future buyer.

I was candid and told the owner that the home could not be listed at that pricing tier unless she was willing to fundamentally redesign it. I recommended that she make some small changes and lower the price by a million dollars. It was still a beautiful home, and buyers in the lower pricing tier would be more forgiving about the structural shortcomings. She could not wrap her head around the market realities and proceeded to make a series of smaller price drops. Four months later, she sold the home for $5.4 million in a short sale and wrote a check to her investors to cover the $600,000 loss.

The owner chased the market all the way to the bottom because she didn't understand the market or consult people who did until it was too late. When she finally solicited the advice of an expert in the market, she couldn't adopt the recommendations because doing so meant admitting failure and coming to grips with her mistakes. She had a psychological attachment to a valuation that was based on nothing other than her imagination.

If you are not selling your home, but are making a large capital investment in your property (a total renovation or ground-up build), do yourself a favor and take those plans to the best-qualified agent in your community to see how the design aligns with the demands of the market. Too many times I have walked into a recently listed newly-finished home, only to think, "My God, why didn't they call me when they were first designing the house? I could have made them so much more money by rearranging some of the rooms, adding a pool, enlarging the great room, or making other modifications to the plans."

# DETAILING DESIGN CHANGES FOR A SELLER

On the initial walk-through with the owner, I make notes about prospective changes to bring the home in alignment with current market predilections. I focus on the renovations that will yield the biggest return on investment. Some are minor cosmetic upgrades—landscaping, paint, fixtures, doors, and hardware; others can be significant structural changes—opening walls to create a great room, raising ceilings to open up a space, or building an island in the kitchen. After I conclude, I meet with the owners and present a detailed marketing proposal that includes the proposed design changes before the home goes up for sale.

## TIME FOR "THE TALK"

Advising a seller how to prepare their home for the market is a delicate conversation, sitting somewhere on the comfort spectrum between a sex talk with a pre-teen and an oncologist's description of a swollen lymph node. Nobody really wants to hear about updating their home, but an agent does a client a disservice by not being completely candid.

I tread lightly and say, "Here are the things I think we need to change. You don't have to do any of them, but if you want to make more money, I strongly recommend it." One walks a fine line between not hurting someone's feelings and making them understand what the public wants.

If the client is open to the possibility of making the changes, I bring in a project manager who charges a fee for the subcontractors to walk through. It takes the project manager two to three weeks to detail to the nickel what the job costs. The client signs the contract with the project manager, sends a deposit, and we are off and running.

The renovations can take anywhere between three weeks and three months.

Renovating a home is an all-or-nothing game. To get into a higher pricing tier, you must go all in. Sellers often make the mistake of cosmetically enhancing their home and leaving one or more rooms untouched due to budgetary constraints or "renovation burnout." It's a costly decision, because buyers will only remember what hasn't been done.

Negative impressions or observations linger longer than positive ones, something bias psychologists call the "negativity effect." Our genetic inheritance predisposes us to pay extra attention to those things in our environment that could harm us. Our brain's capacity to overweight unfavorable information is why that criticism sticks with you more than the compliment, why you forget about the beautiful cocktail dress but fixate on the tear in the seam—or why that aged dishwasher lodges in the memory of a potential buyer even though the rest of the kitchen is updated. Expressed mathematically, good $(+1)$ + bad $(-1)$ = bad $(-1)$.

The seller who leaves outdated rooms will not receive full credit for all the renovation work they did. If 90 percent of the updates are made and 10 percent left undone, the seller won't get 90 percent of the added value of the project if it had been completed. The disproportionate weight of the negative bias reduces the added value significantly.

Most buyers want to turn the key. I frequently hear, "Tracy, we were going to get around to doing that bathroom, but we feel the new owner will likely want to pick out their own finishes." Wrong! That new owner does not want to pick out the finishes, and that new owner is going to pay you far less for the home because you skipped that one space which was a very low percentage of the cost of the work you did, but ended up costing you a lot of money at the time of sale. It's the space the buyers remember!

# STAGING–SHOWING BUYERS HOW TO LIVE IN A HOME

An agent's job in marketing a house is to show prospective buyers how they can live in a house. Most buyers don't visualize a space beyond the way it already looks. They are not conditioned to walk into a home and say, "Look at this space right here. It's not big enough to be our entire living area, but if these two chairs were off-center and we put a small sofa over there, it would open it up." One can show five or six experiences in a house simply through staging and styling.

Staging, the preparation of a home for sale in the marketplace, is the most effective marketing strategy to show buyers the possibilities that exist within a home.

Staging can take many forms: removing clutter, bringing in furniture and art, painting, and even light renovations. Stagers can fill an empty house or accent existing furnishings. Staging can be done piecemeal if the client doesn't have the full budget for it. For example, one might keep an existing dining room table but rent chairs. The living room couch could stay, with rented pillows and a piece of modern art adding touches of coordinated color. Often, it's addition by subtraction where a lot of the existing pieces get removed. Staging emphasizes a property's strengths and minimizes its weaknesses. The preparation process can take several days, but the actual staging is normally done in a single day.

Staging is not just a practical tool to show buyers how to live in a home; it's a form of branding. It reflects a larger cultural trend toward marketing products not just for what they are, but for what they represent. A feeling. A lifestyle. Staging packages a home for potential buyers. It's a presentation designed to engender an emotional response, somewhat analogous to the way Apple packages the iPhone.

In a cluttered and overstimulated world, every part of an iPhone's packaging is carefully conceived to be clean, simple, and elegant. From the moment you pull back the little tab to open the outer box until you peel back the plastic that covers the screen, the process is effortless. No cheap cable ties or bubble wrap. Apple boxes have carefully designed cavities to hold the phone and accessories. The unboxing of a product only happens once, but it leaves a lasting impression, enhancing the product.

The same principle holds true with home staging. Stagers use design elements and concepts that elicit an emotional response in buyers so they can envision a home as their own. The sensory experience that's created in the home and online attracts buyers. Buyers acquire not just the physical property, but the idea of the home presented to them.

To hope that buyers will see beyond clutter or personal elements in a home and grasp its potential is naïve. Do the work for them to facilitate your best possible result.

A recent study[33] by the National Association of Realtors on the impact of home staging revealed:

- 62 percent of sellers' agents say staging a home decreases its time on the market
- 77 percent of buyers' agents say that staging makes it easier for buyers to visualize a property as their future home
- 65 percent of sellers' agents believe staging adds value to a home:

  - 29 percent reported an increase of 1 to 5 percent in dollar value offered by buyers
  - 21 percent reported an increase of 8 to 10 percent
  - 5 percent reported an increase of 11 to 15 percent

The real estate industry would benefit from a more objective and academic study on the relationship between staging and home prices, but in my twenty years of experience, the empirical evidence overwhelmingly supports the claim that sellers who stage homes have a competitive advantage.

## A Mentalist Shows How We Respond to Environmental Suggestions

Derren Brown, an English mentalist and illusionist, wanted to prove how vulnerable we are to subliminal suggestion. He engaged two creative executives from an advertising agency in an experiment. A driver picked the execs up in a town car to meet Brown at a secret location, where Brown proposed an unusual task: come up with a poster advertising a chain of taxidermy stores that included a company name, a slogan, and a visual image. Brown left his own ideas in a sealed envelope on the desk, with the promise that he'd return and open them later.

When Brown returned, the execs revealed their work: a poster for a store called "Animal Heaven," with a large bear standing up, playing a harp, behind the zoo gates to heaven, and the slogan "The best place for dead animals," embellished with a set of angel wings.

Brown then opened the sealed envelope: the poster featured a harp-playing bear, a set of angel wings with the name "Creature Heaven," and the slogan "Where the best dead animals go," zoo gates adorning the background. The similarity was uncanny.

A video showed the execs how Brown had orchestrated the results. The car that picked up the executives followed a prescribed route with carefully placed clues along the way: the London Zoo, a group of children wearing sweatshirts with a graphic image of zoo gates, a "Creature Heaven" sign on a wall, and an image of a harp.

The executives had subliminally noted these images and incorporated them into their campaign.

Brown's experiment demonstrates the influence of our environments over us. Staging is built on a similar principle. Stagers present carefully designed sensory experiences that direct buyers' attention, to help them appreciate a home's attributes and possibilities.

## Can an Interior Designer Stage a Home?

A stager and an interior designer share similarities in that they both select color, fabrics, and furniture to make your home look its best, but there's a critical difference. Designers create a home that reflects your personal tastes and comfort, whereas a stager focuses on making your home appeal to a broad range of tastes. A stager depersonalizes a home. Elements that draw attention to the current occupants of a home are distractions for buyers who are trying to imagine how they might live in that space. Professional stagers have more distance and objectivity to visualize how spaces in a home can be used. They are not hampered by the history or emotional attachments of homeowners. Their consideration is not what has been, but what a home can be.

## Staging Gets Its Own Stage

Any industry that has its own Oscars is likely here to stay. Every year in Las Vegas, the Real Estate Staging Association recognizes artistic excellence in the craft of preparing homes for sale. The categories include Best Occupied Home Stager, Best Vacant Home Stager, and Rising Star. In a move to bring back good taste to award shows, the organizers have shunned the traditional red carpet in favor of a wide plank hardwood walkway with accessory rugs to highlight the décor.

### WHY IT'S ALL WORTHWHILE

Dear Tracy,

We cannot thank you enough for the outcome you delivered on the sale of our home. You, your team, and Robert Federighi, Inc., worked incredibly hard and effectively together to deliver a result that exceeded our expectations in many ways.

We must say that when we met you back in November, we were not sure if our house was a good candidate for your services. After meeting with you we were immediately put at ease and comfortable with the level of attention you would bring to our process. Bringing Bob and his team into the equation was absolutely the right recommendation. When we received the estimate for the work Bob and you recommended, we swallowed hard and put our trust in you and Bob. The results speak for themselves.

Had we listed our house with minimal updates, we estimate our house would have sold for $1,850,000 based on comparable homes sold in Ross in November and December. Further, we believe the level of interest would have been muted and the sales process could have taken significantly longer than it did. With an investment of approximately $200,000, we were thrilled with the offer of $2,450,000 on a no-contingency, all-cash basis and a seven-day close. We honestly could not believe a transaction of that size could come together so quickly that we are still in a bit of shock. The staging by Bob and the pricing by you also worked flawlessly to deliver an outstanding outcome.

We wanted to highlight the specifics of our results because we believe in the specifics of your process and know that endorsements for work well done are more compelling with specific results. Again, we are thrilled with the outcome and will enthusiastically recommend you to any of our friends looking to sell their house in Marin. We are happy to act as a strong reference for you and Bob for any of your prospective clients.

Sincerely,
Jennifer & John

Chapter 4

# TWO PICTURES (BEFORE & AFTER) SAY A THOUSAND WORDS

For years, I tried explaining to my clients the very significant return that staging and pre-listing updating provide at the time of sale, but it's hard to convince sellers. We all struggle to perceive something outside our experience. A seller's resistance to updating and staging a home before it goes on the market is generally anchored in one of four areas: a lack of understanding, the associated expense, a fondness for their home as it is, or a difficulty visualizing the prospective changes to the home.

Homeowners on average sell a home four times during their lifetime. The very infrequency of the experience limits sellers' ability to understand the impact of the measures I recommend, which often take time and cost money. Simultaneously, they are loath to trust someone they may not know very well—their agent—when it comes to undertaking what may be substantial yet discretionary changes.

The expense in and of itself is often deterrent enough. Many homeowners don't have the money, or don't want to assume the expense of renovations prior to listing for sale. Selling real estate should generate capital, not cost, right?

And then we have psychological resistance: people love their homes and don't want to change them. I often remind sellers that staging and renovating do not invalidate the beauty of a home. They are simply strategies to bring a home in line with current market taste. Finally, most people can't visualize what a dramatic impact staging and updating can have. The payoff doesn't seem real or possible.

After years of struggling to impress upon clients the important of pre-sale preparation, I decided to document visually and mathematically the process's efficacy. First, I engage an independent, professional appraiser to evaluate the home before any work is done. I solicit "as is" valuations from several of my very qualified colleagues. The seller then has corroborating accounts of the home's value with their personal finishes, palette, and furniture style. Then, I take "before" pictures. After the project is complete, I take "after" pictures. I meticulously document the exact sum spent on all construction and staging. Finally, the same appraiser and colleagues return to the house to assess value. By the end, my client has not just my expert opinion about before and after value, but also the opinion of other qualified professionals who have represented prospective buyers in their market.

Here's how the numbers work: for every dollar you invest in pre-listing preparation, you get about $3.50 in your pocket. After about ten years of scrupulous documentation, the math has been consistent. This is not a cap, however. Many of the homes I've sold realized a far greater return.

I produced a booklet showcasing the results, and it started to gain traction. People were calling my office to see it from all over the country—Maine, Jackson Hole, and New York. Frustrated sellers with homes sitting on the market, desperate for a solution, send me links to their listings. After review, I send them my analysis on what changes to make for a successful sale. The advice in this book is universal—it applies to every market, whether up or down. Here are a few recent examples.

# | CASE STUDY 1: GET CREATIVE

A homeowner named Gary came into my office despondent that he was not able to sell his property in an upscale suburb north of San Francisco, a community that regularly has sales over ten million dollars. He had unsuccessfully listed it with three brokers for more than two years. The street-to-street, three-acre property had two parcels on it and was beautifully landscaped, with a pool and tennis court on the lower part of the property. The ten-thousand-square-foot residence and outbuildings were on the upper part of the property.

Apart from the narrow buyer pool, this kind of offering has become very difficult to position in today's marketplace. The typical buyer for the home would be a banking or tech executive in his or her thirties. But millennials, no matter how wealthy, don't value excess like previous generations. There are many homes like this that sit idle on the market in places like Greenwich, Connecticut.

According to the American Census Bureau, the average new home has grown by a thousand feet in the past fifty years, and the living space for each person has nearly doubled.[34] But today there are few takers for the ostentatious, leviathan structures that were symbols of the pre-recession boom. Home buyers' attitudes toward conspicuous consumption have changed.

The price of Gary's house had dropped to $13.5 million and it was unlikely the house would sell for more than $12 million as it was. Gary said, "I don't know what to do, Tracy."

I told him, "Here's what you are going to do. We are going to break up your property into two smaller parcels to appeal to buyers shopping in lower price categories, which are selling better. We are going to get plans done. We are going to put story poles up to show people where the new house will be. There's already a pool down at the base of the property where the future home will sit. We are going to get pool plans drawn for your upper house. And we are going to update your home so it has more market appeal."

And that's what we did—we got creative. We had a local "It" architect do renderings of a home on the lower lot. We made cosmetic enhancements and "modernized" many aspects of the existing home on the upper part of the property.

I successfully sold the lower part with the plans for $5 million, and sold the home and the upper part of the lot to...guess who? The largest holder of Bitcoin in the world. *The Wall Street Journal* profiled the sale as an example of how to reposition these types of homes in the marketplace. My seller was thrilled!

Gary's residence had been on the market for a total of 834 days with three different brokerages. The total project cost was $265,575.00 for the improvements, including staging. We listed Gary's updated home and had an accepted offer in 36 days for $10 million. The lower lot, with the architectural plans for a future home, sold for $5 million.

## BEFORE / AFTER

We painted Gary's home gray. A little more than a decade ago, people began gravitating toward a new neutral color for homes. Gray, despite its reputation as being dull, emotionless, and depressed, has emerged as the clear market king. Gray even surpassed beige, the long- standing neutral color titleholder. How did gray do it?

Gray's compatibility with almost every color has made it a go-to exterior and interior color choice for many homeowners. People often think gray is a mix of black and white, but most grays blend in other colors, giving it a versatility that other neutral colors don't offer. And it provides a great backdrop for colorful vegetation.

An analysis by Zillow of 32,000 homes around the country shows that gray homes earn a premium over brown exteriors.[35]

Gray, however, won't last forever as the neutral color du jour in the world of home design. Before gray, brown had a long run as the dominant neutral trend, and sage green preceded brown. Before you decide, consult a professional colorist or designer, or explore the wide array of public resources available to make sure you are choosing the right neutral color for your home.

## BEFORE / AFTER

We changed the multi-use family room to a single-purpose dining area using only staging and paint. We wanted to simplify the experience inside the room. With a dining table shoved into the space and no couch to watch TV, it was not a functional family room. We replaced the table with a smaller, oval one to optimize the space and brought in a more neutral colored rug that revealed the hardwood floors. White paint again provides a cleaner face.

## BEFORE / AFTER

We replaced the dated stone floor in the kitchen that butted up against hardwood floors with a matching dark hardwood. I am not a fan of having a different floor material in a kitchen or foyer that abuts wood or carpet. It makes the room feel choppy and smaller. We added an informal dining table to the end of the island to create a kitchen eat-in space to make it more functional for families.

## BEFORE / AFTER

We converted the sitting room, which has little value in today's market, into a dining room. Simple staging showed buyers how to use the room. Equally important, the room served as a beautiful visual in the marketing of the home on the MLS and in advertisements.

## BEFORE / AFTER

We used splashes of color in the furniture and art, added a chandelier to center the furniture group, and updated the furniture to give the space a more contemporary look.

# CASE STUDY 2: EMPTY HOMES ARE HOUSES

Like many of my clients, Jack was hesitant to update and stage his home before he put it up for sale. He had previously listed the home with another agent who convinced him to repaint and stage the home at a cost of $75,000. Unfortunately, that agent chose the wrong colors and the wrong stager. The house sat on the market for 132 days without an offer. Disillusioned by the response of the market, he rented the home for two years before calling me to sell it. Equal to his skepticism about the expense and the return on investment, he objected to the notion of another stranger imposing his or her taste on his home. He was dubious about the efficacy of staging and wanted to leave the home unfurnished. "Tracy, I wasted $75,000 staging and painting my home and I spent two years playing property manager, not something I wanted to do."

After much discussion, Jack gave me the green light to prep the home for the market with a budget of $175,000.

The market value of the home before updating was $3.6 million. We painted the interior and exterior of the home, installed new hardwood floors and carpet throughout, freshened up the landscaping, and beautifully staged the home. The staging made all the difference! The total project cost, including staging, was $175,700. The home was listed at $4,195,000 and immediately had a whopping offer of $305,000 over the asking price. We closed escrow for $4,500,000. The seller netted a return of $600,000 on capital improvements of $175,000.

It's really unusual for sellers to make post-sale comments on social media. The seller was so thrilled with the results of the sale that he took the liberty of posting about it on Facebook and Instagram.

**Jack Sholl** is with **Tracy McLaughlin**.
May 4 at 3:47 PM · 

Sold!!!!!!!Congratulations and a huge shout out to Tracy McLaughlin. Tracy just sold my house on 13 Acacia Drive, Tiburon for $300,000 over the asking price, with a 21 day close and no contingencies. Unreal.
She took a difficult to position house and made it unbelievably easy. From her recommendations on cosmetic work, dealing with the construction, staging, landscapers and the City of Tiburon.
I highly recommend Tracy. She is a superstar!

TRACYMCLAUGHLIN.COM
**13 Acacia Drive - Tiburon - Sold - Realty - Tracy McLaughlin**

## BEFORE / AFTER

Buyers want to see the architecture of a home before they make an appointment to see it. We removed the excessive vegetation that hid the façade. Cleaning the home up and painting it made it appear new, so it would appeal to younger buyers.

## BEFORE / AFTER

The house was virtually unsellable with the tile flooring from the original construction. We installed wide-planked stained oak floors throughout the home.

## BEFORE / AFTER

People don't buy houses; they buy homes. Walking through an empty room elicits loneliness, not the love and warmth we associate with home. With paint, new carpet, and beautifully scaled furniture, we transformed a cavernous space into an elegant, hotel-like master bedroom.

## BEFORE / AFTER

Most buyers don't visualize how to live inside an empty space. They need to be shown how the room can be used.

Rather than being captivated, people in an empty room will focus on the negative details. *The ceiling design is a little odd. There are no electrical outlets on that wall. The window is too low to put anything in front of it.* We staged the room to divert attention away from its shortcomings.

## BEFORE / AFTER

An empty room does not offer buyers a lifestyle; it creates no emotional connection. By contrast, the furnished living room beckons visitors to come inside.

The gray hardwood flooring and clean white walls made the house feel new, but also allowed the buyer to notice the beautiful bay views through the living room windows.

# CASE STUDY 3: SHINGLE-STYLE RESIDENCE

This ranch-style home in Tiburon, California, was substantially renovated thirteen years earlier but had not been updated since then. A lot happens in the design world over that period of time, and the finishes had fallen out of favor with the target demographic for the house, which was a family with young children. Changes had to be made for the sellers to maximize their equity. The old black, cracked asphalt with weeds growing through it was unsightly and would have been a huge hindrance to maximizing the equity in the home. It was a long, gated driveway with a lot of foreground, so we spent $80,000 of a $306,000 budget on that alone. Now, some might ask, "Why would you spend $80,000 on the driveway of a home you are selling?" Curb appeal. Had we done everything else, and not refinished that driveway in a beautiful gray, classic concrete, the house would have been perceived as a "fixer" the moment a buyer drove in.

An earlier appraisal of this home was in the $2.8 million range "as is." The total project cost, including staging, was $306,250. My clients netted a total of $895,000 from the capital improvements.

## BEFORE / AFTER

Shingle-style homes are one of the most uniquely American types of architecture, and buyers gravitate toward the traditional New England gray exterior. We painted the brown shingles gray to make the house look new and to appeal to buyers' tastes.

## BEFORE / AFTER

With every project, homeowners must decide which changes are absolutely essential and which can be cheated. The beat-up driveway had to be replaced with clean concrete, even though it consumed 26 percent of our budget. We weren't going to fix up the house and have people enter on a dilapidated driveway. It would distort the lens through which they subsequently viewed the home. We removed the rotted front deck, saving money by not replacing it. In California, people don't tend to spend time on front decks. They prioritize being in the backyard where the family gathers. Instead, we expanded the lawn to roll right up to the house, making the front yard that much larger and lending vibrancy to the exterior. The final touch was a beautiful, contemporary staircase leading to the front door.

## BEFORE / AFTER

Here, an out-of-style formless space is transformed into a sophisticated, contemporary living room with simple paint and staging changes. A neutral white color has many benefits. It not only makes a room appear larger, but also creates the perfect backdrop for your art collection. White confers cleanliness, freshness, and simplicity. It also maximizes the natural light in the room, enhancing reflectivity.

## BEFORE / AFTER

Simple changes—paint, a lighting fixture, a new area rug, and furniture—convert a stuffy, old-fashioned space into a chic and comfortable dining area. Once again, we brightened the interior with white wall paint and a light-colored rug. We chose a modern light encasement with a simple geometric shape and staged the room with a more inviting dining table and sumptuously upholstered chairs. Modern art frames the space and adds a splash of color. The shades of blue brighten the room and coordinate with colors throughout the house.

## BEFORE / AFTER

Minimal changes transformed an oppressive, monochromatic wood kitchen into an open, modern space that's the hub of the home. We painted the cabinets and replaced the island barstools. We did not alter the counters, backsplash, hardwood floors, or knobs. Painting the cabinets white makes the backsplash "pop." Look at the difference a coat of paint makes! If we had had a larger budget, we might have darkened the floors, but painting the interior walls and kitchen cabinets made them feel more modern.

## BEFORE / AFTER

Addition by subtraction. We converted a cramped, cluttered TV area to a light, stripped-down workspace. Decluttering a room frees up mental space for buyers, allowing them to imagine themselves living in a home.

# CASE STUDY 4: WATERFRONT RESIDENCE

The owners traveled through Bali and Indonesia and brought home beautiful objets d'art, furniture, and trees. They wanted to infuse the magic of those regions into their waterfront residence. Sometimes, though, what's experienced on vacation should stay on vacation.

Rather than being hypnotized by the swirling Balinese fans and the lush tropical vegetation, the mishmash of design styles would distract prospective buyers from the beauty of the property. So we stripped those elements away and brought forward the best qualities of the home.

A pre-renovation appraisal of this home was $3.8 million "as is." After many meetings with the owners, I decided the budget was best spent by doing the following: staining the hardwood floors, interior and exterior paint, replacing all rotted exterior doors and windows, refacing the kitchen, adding two new bathrooms and a new floor in the third bathroom, new carpet, new lighting, and substantial landscape improvements; the total project cost, including staging, was $306,250. The house sold for $4,695,000! My clients netted $588,750 over the appraisal price as a result of the capital improvements.

## BEFORE / AFTER

Picking the right color for a home's exterior is critical. The blue-gray exterior paint lacked the sophistication for a stately home, so we painted it a more traditional shade of "straight gray."

The grounds should reflect the architectural style of the home. The property was overgrown with palms and large tropical plants that had no connection to the area or the home design. We replaced the

Balinese-style plants and trees in favor of a more traditional, New England-style garden to appeal to the demographic that typically buys homes on the Belvedere Lagoon.

The original flagstone in the entryway was peppered with reds and browns—colors that did not correspond to the palette of the home. To save money, we painted the flagstone gray instead of replacing it.

## BEFORE / AFTER

The blond wood floors, despite their ability to brighten up a space and hide dirt, have fallen out of favor, so we stained them dark.

We painted the interior blue walls a neutral white. Pale blue purportedly slows human metabolism and has a calming effect, which is why it often shows up in bedrooms and bathrooms; however, it damps the energy of a public space and is a poor showcase for art.

The Chinese lanterns were fun, but not in line with the style of the home. They hung far down from the ceiling, which pulled the eye down and diverted attention away from the incredible high ceilings and scale of the foyer and stairwell.

The oversized foyer was dead space, so we added value by creating an informal dining area. We chose the Slim Aaron pool photograph for its water relief and as a balance to the lagoon waters outside the backyard doors.

## BEFORE / AFTER

We reconfigured the kitchen layout. We removed the peninsula that bisected the room and installed an island to open up traffic flow and bring the outdoors into the kitchen. We updated the appliances, added lighting above the island, changed the kitchen slabs and backsplash, and refaced the cabinets.

## BEFORE / AFTER

Natural or exposed wood has very little appeal for women in the current marketplace, particularly in a master bedroom. We were lucky that we had high ceilings to work with. We changed the sconces over the bed, painted the ceiling and walls, and replaced the carpet.

# CASE STUDY 5: REPOSITIONING AN EAST COAST HOME ON THE WEST COAST

As our digitally interconnected lives become more demanding and hectic, people increasingly look toward a more relaxed, easy way of living inside their homes. Here, we took a colonial-style home with finishes that were overly formal for today's market and gave it an injection of youthfulness. The changes included landscaping, removing shutters, interior paint, updated lighting, staining the hardwood floors, refacing the kitchen cabinets, and full staging.

The original market value was $3.6 million before any constructive improvements were made. The total project cost was $214,445. The home was listed at $3,995,000, had a preemptive offer before scheduled offers were to be received, and closed at $4,200,000. My clients netted a total of $385,555 from a capital investment of $214,445.

## BEFORE / AFTER

We removed the decorative black shutters to make the home less colonial and more of a contemporary farmhouse.

We manicured the landscaping to bring more color and contrast to the front of the house. The inexpensive black decorative mulch not only is good for the plants, but also frames the green hedge and provides a clean definition for the house.

## BEFORE / AFTER

Brown, brown, brown. The wall color combined with the silver ceiling made the room feel closed-in. As with other examples, white paint transformed the space. We exchanged the low-hanging chandelier in the dining room for a higher drum fixture that pulls the eye up and makes the ceiling feel more expansive. We traded the carpet for hardwood floors that match the rest of the house.

## BEFORE / AFTER

Again, shades of brown made this small space feel claustrophobic. We swapped the wall color for a neutral white to make the room appear larger, selected a sexy chandelier to optimize ceiling height, and added hardwood floors. Once dated and drab, the office now feels like a space in a boutique hotel.

## BEFORE / AFTER

Structurally, nothing was wrong with the original kitchen, but it was bland and forgettable. We stained the hardwood floors a darker color for contrast and richness and painted the walls white. We also refaced the dated cabinets with simple Shaker-style cabinets, and changed the lighting over the island and dining space. Finally, we staged the room with more contemporary chairs, barstools, and a glass table to bring it into the modern era.

# CASE STUDY 6: SAN FRANCISCO TOWNHOME

This 4,810-square-foot single-family dwelling in San Francisco's Marina District was completely renovated (down to the studs) in 2006. Twelve years later, the renovation showed signs of age that would preclude it from selling for top dollar. The neighborhood typically trades to families and tech executives, a demographic that wants less formality and more chic, simple, and clean-lined finishes. Simple palette changes in the interior, exterior, and floor colors and some bathroom updating, along with the styling and staging, created $1 million in additional value for these sellers.

## BEFORE

## AFTER

The original color, a blue/gray palette, was acceptable, but the tonality of the gray did not optimize the marketability of a $5 million home that trades to a sophisticated buyer who is likely in their forties and wants a more tailored, sophisticated look.

Look at the difference a new front door, new garage door, and new paint color makes. The windows were not changed, but the simple exterior changes make it look like "new construction."

## BEFORE / AFTER

While we all loved maple finishes in 2006, they now date a home. It's hard for sellers to understand how painting out or staining lighter woods like maple makes such a difference in the optics of marketing, but it does.

This looks like a new penthouse. The white paint, new door hardware, and darker stain on the floor create a "new construction" look. The entry is the first thing buyers see and often what they remember most, so efforts here provide an enormous return on investment.

## BEFORE / AFTER

The main level of this home suffered from a generic palette that provided no contrast for photos or marketing. Look at the difference the darkened hardwood floors and wall color make in the main living space!

## BEFORE / AFTER

The powder room, an opportunity to showcase high design, had a bland palette, dated pedestal sink, and lighting with no "punch."

Buyers love chic powder rooms. They are an opportunity to "play" and have fun with design! We chose a very current wall covering, new vanity and fixtures, and new mirror to transform the room! The powder room set the tone for the changes we made to the rest of the home.

## BEFORE / AFTER

Consistent flooring is key to a more marketable look and higher price for sellers. I am constantly removing stone, marble, and tile floors in rooms, like this kitchen, that abut other main spaces, to create a cohesive flow and continuity that is mandatory for a higher price. I removed the marble flooring from the kitchen and ran the hardwoods into that room for cohesion. Look at the difference in the shot with hardwood flooring and new paint!

## BEFORE / AFTER

The living room only needed new wall color and new floor stain. Those two simple changes, coupled with our high-end staging, created a "brand-new penthouse" look and feel!

## BEFORE / AFTER

The kitchen was a bit dated. It had more of an early 2000s modern feeling, which is a bit harsh for this market. We did not have the budget to gut the entire kitchen, so we simply changed the wall color and brought in new hardwood flooring, which we stained to match the existing flooring, and the kitchen was immediately updated.

## BEFORE / AFTER

Simple paint changes, the staining of the hardwood floors, and removal of a surface mount fixture that was unnecessary where it was, coupled with the staging, transformed the family room off the kitchen.

## BEFORE / AFTER

## BEFORE / AFTER

We replaced the stress-inducing persimmon wall color with clean white walls, removed the garish light fixture, and brought the room into the modern era.

## BEFORE / AFTER

This master bathroom had a real "1990s Vegas" feeling to it. The extensive use of busy high-gloss marble and the non-utilitarian double vanity with no storage were not marketable. In an ideal world, the bathroom would have been entirely replaced. However, due to budgetary constraints, I made the decision to replace just the existing marble floor with a porcelain tile floor that complemented the existing marble, and I replaced the vanity.

## BEFORE / AFTER

This secondary family room, or "rec room," had dated elements. The change of wall color, staining of the floors, and staging created a "brand-new" experience for the buyers.

## BEFORE / AFTER

While the existing bathroom was very functional and generally acceptable to buyers, it wouldn't sell at the highest possible price due to the palette and finishes. The vanity is also non-utilitarian with no storage.

We replaced the blue wall and floor tile with a more contemporary, desirable porcelain tile and replaced the vanity and mirror. Voilà, a new bathroom!

## BEFORE / AFTER

The master bedroom had great scale, but felt dated and dark due to dark walls and blond floors. For the "new" look, we stained the floors, painted the walls, and staged. The room looks brand-new. It's not!

## BEFORE / AFTER

## BEFORE / AFTER

## BEFORE / AFTER

Sellers often forget the importance of landscaping. Having a flat, usable backyard in the hilly topography of San Francisco is very valuable. However, this yard was not being optimized in terms of usability or appearance. Simply rolling out the new turf and staging created a usable, appealing yard.

Chapter 5

# DISCLOSE, PERMIT, INSPECT

an Galai and Orly Sade of the Hebrew University of Jerusalem coined the term "ostrich effect" in 2006 to describe investors' tendency to block out negative financial information during difficult times. The moniker comes from the pervasive but false belief that ostriches bury their heads in the sand during times of danger. Instead of confronting a situation that threatens them and pushing through the attendant anxiety, people will underestimate the likelihood of a bad outcome and its effects on their life and property. For people with this cognitive bias, often the fact of never having experienced a particular situation before serves as anecdotal evidence justifying their belief that the situation will therefore never occur.

In residential real estate, the ostrich effect consistently surfaces in two areas: the disclosure of defects in a home and the permitting of home improvements. People wishfully believe that they can circumvent the rules without repercussion. However, failure to permit or to disclose problems with a property carries great financial and emotional costs.

# IN THE INTEREST OF FULL DISCLOSURE

In 2013, Derek and Maria Broaddus, a young couple with three children, purchased their 3,920-square-foot dream home in in a wealthy suburb thirty miles from Manhattan. Three days after closing the sale for $1.3 million, they received a letter from someone calling himself "the Watcher." "My grandfather watched the house in the 1920s, and my father watched it in the 1960s," the letter said. "It is now my turn." It was the first of three letters they received in the summer of 2014. The Watcher continued, "I am pleased to now know your names and the names of the young blood you have brought me." Not exactly a warm loaf of bread and a bottle of wine. Welcome to the neighborhood.

The Broadduses never moved into the house. Instead, they filed a lawsuit against the original owners for failure to disclose that they had received a letter from the Watcher and "suppressed material facts in connection with the sale of the home." After three years of litigation, the judge eventually dismissed the lawsuit, but not before the buyer and seller spent three years and thousands of dollars debating what, if anything, the original owners knew, and what they were compelled to share with the buyers. In real estate, sellers have a legal obligation to disclose past and current problems to potential buyers, but the Broaddus case touched on the complex question: exactly how far does the obligation go?

All states require sellers to issue some form of property disclosure statement that acknowledges defects in the property for sale. States mandate disclosures so buyers can make informed decisions about a property. The laws vary from state to state, and sometimes from city to city. Massachusetts, for example, operates under the principle of *caveat emptor*, Latin for "buyer beware."[36] The buyer assumes the risk of the purchase, and the seller has no obligation to acknowledge known defects of the property. If snow pours through the roof every winter or visitors disappear in the quicksand behind the shed, buyers must unearth the problems on their own.

Sellers must fully disclose what they know only if specifically asked about an issue. By contrast, California has extremely stringent disclosure requirements.[37] The seller and seller's agents must provide a transparent picture of not just the structure and the land, but also the surrounding area and any other factors that might adversely affect the property's value or sale. Sellers must disclose not just the sinking foundation and 6.0 earthquake that rocked their home; they must also reveal less tangible, psychological defects, like the incessant barking of the neighbor's dog, or the man who mysteriously died in the basement two years earlier.

## Disclosure Litmus Test

Going beyond the compulsory laws, the litmus test I use for disclosures is: "If I were a buyer, is this issue something I'd want to know about?" If yes, disclose it. You can rarely go wrong by being forthright. Although the revelation of problems can feel threatening to a seller, buyers who are emotionally invested in a home generally won't walk away. The "oversharing" can actually advantage sellers, because buyers are disarmed by the honesty.

The seller's short-term anxiety around disclosure pales in comparison to the long-term stress arising from failure to disclose property defects. A series of studies on secrets in the Journal of Personality and Social Psychology shows that the stress of hiding something comes not from the act of concealment, but from how often we think about the secret.[38] The authors suggest that when we keep a secret, we actually establish a goal to keep the information secret. We can never fully accomplish the goal because the possibility of discovery is ongoing, so our mind perseverates on it. According to research, continually revisiting the information we have secreted in the dark recesses of our mind's filing cabinets adversely impacts our feelings of authenticity, well-being, and physical health.

Non-disclosure is the single biggest source of residential lawsuits. Most people who don't disclose something material get caught. Homes are surrounded by neighbors who hear things and talk. Former owners or renters resurface. The contractor who did the unpermitted construction last year may be engaged by the new owner post-closing and describe the previous work to them. Non-disclosure is the sword that hangs above the homeowner's head while living in the home, during escrow, and after the sale closes.

I meticulously go through every line on a disclosure form with my clients who are sellers to ensure its compliant and appropriate completion. I require that prospective buyers sign to attest that they have read and approve of the entire packet, including disclosures, in connection with any offer they submit. I don't want them tying up the house and renegotiating the price later.

# ▌ PERMITS

When homeowners want to make constructive changes to a property, they must apply for a permit with the local government agency. Local agencies have building codes to provide reasonable assurance that a home is safe from structural failure, fire hazards, dangerous electrical and heating systems, electric shock, and health risks. The permitting process also provides a permanent record of the work performed and inspections conducted on the project.

Getting a permit may seem costly and time-consuming, but the consequences can be considerable if you build or renovate without approval.

I represented the sale of a beautiful home that sat at the end of a long, winding driveway. A few years earlier, the owners had hired a contractor who built an addition to the house without pulling permits. At the time, the family was expecting a baby and wanted to save the time, money, and hassle of getting the permit. Operating under the presumption that "it's easier to ask for forgiveness than permission," the owners thought they could always pull the permits retroactively if there were ever an issue.

Before the house went on the market, I encouraged the owners to redress the problem and get the property properly permitted. They refused. Much like years earlier, they wanted to move quickly and not be ensnared in red tape.

In California, by law, any unpermitted work must be disclosed to buyers. When the property was put up for sale, the owners disclosed to the buyer that the work was completed without a permit. During the escrow period, the buyer went to the city inspection office to find out what would be required to turn the addition into a legal structure.

When the city stepped in, not only did the owners have to retroactively permit the addition, but they had to permit it to "current code." The code had changed a year earlier to require homes with long driveways and without easy fire access to have their own fire hydrant. Consequently, the owners had to pull up their $200,000 driveway to run a water line beneath it from the public street to their home. The unforeseen costs of not originally permitting the addition were astronomically higher than they ever imagined.

The bottom line: renovation and construction should be done with permits. The capital improvements of unpermitted work will never be valued the same as permitted work. It doesn't matter if the quality of construction would outlast the Pyramid of Giza. Unless an inspector reviews and signs off on your improvement, and there's a permit trail to prove it, the market will mercilessly discount the unpermitted work, if you can find a buyer for your property at all.

People flout permit laws to save time and money, but end up spending more time and money fixing the problem they create. You either pay as you go, or pay severely when you try to sell your home. Failure to get proper permits is a mistake that can negate a lot of the value a seller has added to a home. It's a potential liability, a blemish, a dark cloud, and a nightmare for everyone.

## The Top Ten Reasons to Obtain Permits for Constructive Improvements

10. You may owe back taxes for the difference between the existing square footage and the newly assessed footage.

9. A homeowner's policy may not cover unpermitted sections of the home.

8. Penalties often attach to unpermitted work.

7. You may suffer the costs of conforming to a new, more stringent set of building codes.

6. You may have to restore the home to its pre-renovation state.

5. You're at the mercy of government building inspectors who can make the remediation process hellish for homeowners who are in violation.

4. Unpermitted work needs to be disclosed to potential buyers, so the truth will come out, and so buyers will not assume any associated cost or liability.

3. Unpermitted homes sell for less than equivalent homes with permits.

2. Peace of mind.

1. Karma.

# ▍PRE-LISTING INSPECTIONS

After years of watching deals get canceled or substantially renegotiated after buyers complete their inspections, I have made it a policy in my office that sellers who are working with me must have their homes thoroughly inspected prior to listing them. Approximately one in twenty sales contracts blow up on the road to closing and, apart from financing, home inspections are the primary cause of deals being delayed or falling apart.[39]

In California, the wide-ranging but necessary inspections include a general home inspection; roof inspection; foundation inspection with a licensed structural engineer; sewer lateral inspection; drainage inspection; well, septic, and chimney/fireplace inspections; and pool and spa inspection. Buyers need to sign off on these before I accept offers. Depending on the characteristics of the house, the following additional inspections may be required:

- Pest Inspection
- Tree/Arborist Inspection
- Structural Inspection
- Mold Inspection

If the owner wants to remediate problems before bringing the house to market, we do that. At the very least, all the issues related to the property will be made known, and offers will be predicated on the prospective buyers' knowledge and acceptance of the reports and the seller's disclosures. This is the best possible investment a seller can make in a home. If a seller's escrow is canceled, it generally costs them a fortune, as it is impossible to recapture the momentum.

The purpose of a pre-listing inspection is to greatly reduce the costly possibility of a home falling out of contract due to the discovery of previously unknown issues. A pre-listing inspection prevents the buyer from coming back and renegotiating the price. Buyers can still commission their own inspection, but they've signed off on everything in our disclosure packet, limiting their ability to renegotiate.

Buyers will frequently request a one-day contingency to review the house with their own contractor to verify disclosures in the report. In that case, I don't change the listing status from "for sale" to "pending" so the listing doesn't get tarnished if the buyer backs out during that short period.

The minute a house goes off the market during a contingency period, especially if it remains off-market for two or three weeks, a seller likely loses all other buyers, a cost far greater than the money the seller would have spent on inspections. The initial listing momentum evaporates, not to be regained, and the house is blemished.

When there's no inspection contingency and buyers are willing to sign off on the house, it greatly improves the prospects of closing. If you can sell the house the day you accept the offer, there's no better position to be in.

But a pre-listing inspection doesn't protect a buyer from every exigency.

## Who You Gonna Call?

I listed a home for $4.5 million, an unusually high sale price for this home's particular area. We had all the inspections done before the house went on the market. Immediately, we received an offer $100,000 over asking. The buyer went into contract at $4.6 million and signed off on everything. She was travelling and asked for one week to verify inspections. It was such a strong offer that we agreed.

The next week the woman showed up with a crew and a machine I'd never seen. I said, "What's that?" She said, "I'm testing for electromagnetic field radiation. I'm concerned that the presence of electric currents—from power lines, transformers, appliances, faulty wiring—could pose a risk to human health." Ghostbusters also use electromagnetic field (EMF) meters to test for apparitions.

Her team ran their EMF tests and she didn't like the readings. She brought in another expert who came up with a lower reading. She asked for an extension, which we gave her because, by then, we had lost the other interested parties. We were off the market for two full weeks. She tried to dramatically renegotiate the price and we refused.

She canceled the deal, saying, "I can't live with EMFs." I quietly wondered how a lower sale price would have remediated the electromagnetic fields.

In twenty years of working in real estate, I had only run into EMF testing once before, and that time it was legitimate—there was a transponder on the property generating EMFs.

We were dead in the water going into Memorial Day weekend. I called the owner and said, "We have to do something dramatic. Lower the house by $500,000." My hope was to get multiple offers and push it back up to $4.3 million. If we sat there at $4.5 million, we would be at a huge disadvantage.

We lowered the price and got three offers immediately. Guess who wrote one of the offers: the EMF lady. She must have had a magnetic attraction to the property. We sold the house to another buyer for $4.3 million, but her little EMF exercise cost my client around $200,000.

Chapter 6

# MARKETING AND BRANDING A HOME

*"You do not really understand something unless you can explain it to your grandmother."*

**–Albert Einstein**

A ttention is a scarce commodity in the twenty-first century. Everything competes for your attention. Commercials, print ads, brand labels, Facebook notifications, Twitter, Instagram, the Groupon ad that's going to save you 90 percent at the flying trapeze class, that tweet, the Fortnite story in your newsfeed, Mom's email that's sitting in your inbox, the school fundraiser, the file your boss just dropped on your desk, the estate sale that just popped up on Nextdoor—they all want you to stop and pay attention.

If you're selling a home in our hyper-digitalized and noisy world, how do you make people pay attention? How does it stand out from the competition? How do you get buyers to remember your home?

Brand it.

Branding a home is the key to cutting through the clutter.

Brought to the New World from Spain, branding started as a practice where ranchers burned a mark on cattle to signify ownership. Guarding against loss or thievery on open ranches, the brands had to be simple, unique, and easily identifiable. Modern marketers conscripted the term to describe the practice of giving a product an identity that distinguished it from otherwise nearly indistinguishable competitors. But a brand in today's world goes far beyond a utilitarian identification symbol. A brand is the *perception* that someone has when they hear or think of a product or service. The perception is the brand. When you buy an iPhone, you're not just buying a device that allows you to talk, text, email, and take photographs. You're buying into Apple's core conviction that "creative people with passion can change the world for the better."[40] You, more likely than not, identify with this creed. You are now part of a tribe that would say it "thinks different," and that values good taste, aesthetics, and simplicity.

As described by consumer psychologist Peter Noel Murray, a brand "is nothing more than a mental representation of a product in the consumer's mind. If the representation consists only of the product's attributes, features, and other information, there are no emotional links to influence consumer preference and action."[41] A brand creates an emotional connection between a product and a consumer, a buyer and a seller.

In the simplest terms, a brand is what you think of when you hear a brand name.

# ▌ STORYTELLING

*"We tell ourselves stories in order to live."*

—**Joan Didion**[42]

Branding is built on a narrative that has a beginning, a middle, and an end—a story line that creates an emotional connection with a buyer. Great stories are easy to grasp. They simplify complex ideas, so they stick in people's minds. In a world inundating us with information, our brains desperately search for narratives to lend coherence.

Jennifer Aaker, a Stanford behavioral psychologist and professor of marketing, says, "When most people advocate for an idea, we think of a compelling argument, a fact or a figure. But research shows that our brains are not hardwired to understand logic and facts for very long. Our brains are wired to understand and retain stories. A story is a journey that moves the listener, and when the listener goes on that journey they feel different and the result is persuasion and sometimes action."[43]

We continually tell ourselves stories to organize and make sense of our lives. Contradictions and inconsistencies are disregarded, and the story becomes the truth that was lived. *This is where I grew up. This is how my fiancé and I met. This is how our marriage survived the challenges. This was my career path.* The stories we create about ourselves don't just shape our identities, they are our identities—and the principle also holds true with homes.

We can control the story of our homes. When I accept a listing, my first step is to develop a story around the home. *What is this home going to represent in the marketplace? What are the keywords, photographs, and descriptive language that will define it? What do I want the buyer to think, feel, and do in response to the story? Why would people who hear the story want to share it with others?*

Most agents don't think of branding a home. They use very generic language—nondescript, recycled lines that just become part of the cultural noise. They don't grab people's attention.

I recently had a nondescript listing. I didn't have much to say about the house but, when I squinted, it reminded me of a Pasadena home. Instead of just writing, "Lovely flat yard, pool, indoor-outdoor living," I framed the house as "reminiscent of the iconic *Father of the Bride* film with Steve Martin." Many people read and commented on that description online. At the Sunday open house, I several times overheard home shoppers murmur: "Yes, this does seem like Pasadena." "I feel like I'm in that movie."

People will buy into your narrative if you present it in a compelling way. You must introduce an idea, rooted in the truth, that people will believe and remember. In the remembering lies the branding. "Great open floor plan" is a bland and boring pitch. By referencing *Father of the Bride* instead, I distinguished the listing from the other $2.2 million homes on the market, enabling buyers to identify and remember it.

Some might question whether the simple tagline, "reminiscent of the iconic *Father of the Bride* film with Steve Martin" tells a "story." Unequivocally, yes. The story that I borrowed for the branding of the home was not the literal narrative of a father grappling with the challenges of his daughter getting married, but the *feeling* evoked by the film—of family and love inside a charming, warm suburban home. That's the lens though which buyers viewed and talked about the home.

I construct a narrative around each listing, a story that communicates the essence of the home, what differentiates it, and why the buyer should care.

I represented a sprawling twenty-five-year-old home in Tiburon, California, a holdover from the McMansion era, that was very difficult to position in the marketplace. It lacked any outward appeal and did not align with market preferences. It was 6,200 square feet, but had no yard—a family home that wasn't really a family home. The house had soaring ceilings with formal columns, a style completely out of vogue in the current market. The home had not been updated. We did $200,000 in capital improvements to make it visually more appealing. Now it was time to come up with a brand.

The brand concept was a challenge given the architectural constraints of the home. But, if you think long and hard enough, an idea always emerges. I was ruminating about the great, stately homes in *Architectural Digest* and the brand materialized: "Straight out of *Architectural Digest*." People know the publication. The association inherently elevated the otherwise ordinary, and in some ways problematic, home in the minds of the buyers. It wasn't a misleading brand, because that style of home was once very popular in *Architectural Digest*. The tagline gave buyers a simple way to conceptualize the home in a favorable light.

We closed the deal with a buyer who had flown from Connecticut to San Francisco to meet with his new company and find a home before moving across the country. He had looked at fifteen or twenty homes in four different neighborhoods in the city, including our Tiburon listing. He boarded his plane home with a screaming two-year-old, dizzy from the prospect of relocating his family across the country, transitioning kids into a new school, and the emotional disruption that comes with moving. Most of the time, buyers depart homes without a firm recollection of the property or layout. But this buyer remembered the home that was straight out of *Architectural Digest*. The label provided a handle he could carry back to the East Coast. The all-cash sale closed in fourteen days.

The quality of the product comes first when creating an identity for a home. Good branding won't obviate the need for updates and renovations. As discussed in chapter 5, get your home in the best possible shape before you put it on the market. Branding is not just about excellent marketing strategies, tricking people, or convincing buyers that they want something they don't. To the contrary, you can never mislead the consumer. But you can take a glass that's half empty and make it appear half full through creative branding. And you can always conceive of something that resonates with home shoppers and lends the home a distinct identity. That's all branding is.

# I FEEL THEREFORE I BUY: EMOTIONS DRIVE DECISION-MAKING

Scientific research now shows that we feel first and think second. Our senses process information much faster than our cognitive brain computes the same information. Emotion plays as much of a role in a buyer's decision to purchase as does rational logic. Buyers are more responsive to emotional and psychological appeals than to empirical data about a property's features or functions.

Neuroscientist Antonio Damasio studied people who had lost parts of their frontal cortex—and their ability to feel emotion. His primary case study was a highly intelligent, professionally successful man he pseudonymously called Elliot.

Surgeons had to remove a brain tumor from Elliot. After the surgery, Elliot's reasoning and logic functioned normally, but the procedure left him incapable of feeling emotions. "I never saw a tinge of emotion in my many hours of conversation with him: no sadness, no impatience, no frustration," Damasio wrote in his groundbreaking book, *Descartes' Error*.[44] The impact of the surgery on Elliot's emotions was not unexpected, but it opened up a surprising revelation.

The obvious inference is that Eliot's tragic loss of emotion should afford a silver lining of improved, hyper-rational cognitive process. The traditional view is that the best decisions come from a calm, cool head, devoid of emotions. In theory, Elliot's professional life therefore should have fired on all cylinders, because emotion no longer disturbed his thinking and decision-making capabilities.

In fact, the opposite was true. Elliot's professional life fell apart. Rather than becoming perfectly rational, Elliot was paralyzed by indecision. Without access to his emotions, Elliot was incapable of making judgments. He could think clearly, but lacked any sense of how he felt about his options. Elliot's lack of emotion made it impossible for him to perceive more value in one choice over another.

Damasio's research upended our culture's long-held belief that reason and emotion sit in opposition to each other. Neuroscience now recognizes that emotion is inextricably intertwined with reason in the decision-making process.

As described by Jennifer Lerner, a Harvard professor who studies the relationship between emotions and decision-making, "emotions powerfully, predictably, and pervasively influence decision-making."[45] When humans experience an emotion, they are instinctively driven to action.

Buyers and sellers must acknowledge the importance of emotions in the decision-making process so they can formulate branding, marketing, and acquisition strategies that facilitate and take account of emotional drives. Buyers may analyze and compare the price, square footage, the number of bedrooms and bathrooms, the length of their potential commute, the finishes, and the prices of comparative properties, but walking into a home and experiencing an emotional connection trumps all. As Damasio's research illustrates, buyers' decision to make an offer, despite rational analysis of empirical attributes and alternatives, is inextricably linked to how they feel.

As Maya Angelou once said, "I've learned that people will forget what you said, people will forget what you did, but people will never forget how you made them feel." The same can be said for the home you buy.

## Keeping Emotions in Check

To keep emotions from hijacking decision-making and blinding us to practical considerations, buyers can create a rubric with the elements of a home they value the most. Keep it simple and pick a manageable number of criteria to grade. Use a traditional point scale, and assign point values to each feature so they total 100.

A rubric might look something like this:

- Location/20
- Number of Bedrooms/15
- Number of Bathrooms/10
- Size of Outdoor Flat Pad/15
- School District/10
- Price/15
- Walking Distance to Town/5
- Pool/5
- Separate Office/5

Then go through and give point values to each feature of a particular house you are considering.

Home shoppers won't buy a home solely based on a metric, but the grading exercise provides more objectivity. If nothing else, you will have tipped your cap to the Age of Analytics and Data.

# ▌ BRANDING TOOLS

Branding a home starts with the home's description in the Multiple Listing Service (MLS). The MLS is a locale-specific database for brokers representing sellers to share information about their listed properties with brokers who are representing buyers. There are roughly nine hundred separate MLS systems in the United States.

The digital age has changed the MLS. Only brokers used to see MLS listings. Now, it's more of a consumer marketplace, where limited listings can be viewed by anyone looking for a home. Most MLS systems syndicate their data to national real estate portals like Zillow and Trulia. The growing number of online platforms specializing in real estate has diminished the preeminence of the MLS, but it's still the top hub for residential real estate. The MLS is considered the most accurate and reliable of the home search websites because the brokers must abide by strict rules and the information is input by the agent representing the seller.

Choosing which words will appear in the MLS listing is key to defining the brand of your home. You must emphasize the words that will attract your target audience, starting with a captivating headline. In the MLS headline, don't sell the product; sell a lifestyle or the feeling the home engenders. A headline like "Motivated Seller" is not what dreams are made of. "Balinese Retreat in the Hills Above San Francisco Bay" is more likely to garner attention.

The word count for the description of the property varies by MLS, but it's generally less than a hundred. The words and images that are loaded into the MLS are the foundation of the narrative about a home. Use the words to shape the identity, or brand, of the home that you want to lodge in a buyer's mind.

The adage "a picture is worth a thousand words" holds true for photos on the MLS, and on a property's individual website. Buyers are more apt to judge your home based on the photos than the description. Having great photos to showcase your home is critical. If you are not a professional photographer, hire one. The expenditure will pay for itself several times over.

The sequencing of the photos is important. The first photo is the "money" shot. Start on the outside. If the front exterior is unattractive, find a reverse shot of the back. The image could be a nearby lagoon, even if your house isn't on it. The image must make buyers click a second time. Depending on the property, additional angles of the exterior may be warranted. Then, you walk the potential buyer through the home. Sequence the photos the way you'd walk through and live in the house. The goodbye shot looks back at the gate, driving away.

Supporting video is a useful tool if the home is worthy of it, but people have short attention spans with the marketing of homes. They will not watch a virtual tour or a long video. Consumers want quick edits that allow them to visually digest the information quickly.

# SOCIAL MEDIA AND PROPERTY VOYEURISM

Social media is an essential tool to market and brand your home. There's no better way to get a home into your sphere of influence—and it's free.

A study by New York University, Harvard, and Facebook economists showed that property buying decisions are strongly influenced by a person's social media networks.[46] Analyzing data from Facebook, the research found that individuals who had friends in another city that experienced a significant rise in home values were more likely to transition from renting to owning in their hometown, even though they lived in a completely different market. If housing investment decisions are influenced by social media networks across cities, it's safe to assume that the impact of social media networks is significant within local markets.

The social media content must add value to people's lives, or they won't engage. In the modern social-network era, people's attention must be earned, not bought. The traditional model of blasting one-way messages doesn't work anymore. People have tremendous choice over how, when, and where to place their attention. If traditional marketing were analogous to giving a speech, today marketing is more akin to hosting a dinner gathering. If you are a marketer, you better bring something to the table, or there won't be a seat for you. A "Home for Sale" sign passing through a news feed won't get much consideration. A good broker will leverage his or her community and contacts in the service of selling your home. I post every listing I am representing on my social media, but posting listings is not enough.

The local members of social networks generally have an inherent interest in real estate. They either own or rent a property in that market, so housing and values in the community are relevant to them. The key is converting that interest into attention.

Home sellers can leverage social communities by creating content that recognizes that people are the medium, not just the market. People look for content that can be shared with their communities. If you provide something of value, they'll reciprocate by forwarding it to someone or posting it for their four hundred friends. According to Nielson research, 92 percent of consumers trust word-of-mouth and recommendations from friends and family above all other forms of advertising.[47]

Social media is an informal platform for reaching out to people and telling them why I love a house so much. I can talk to people conversationally, and people relate to it.

The packaging of the content captures the attention of people beyond buyers. Not all the homes I sell are beautiful, but we make them look beautiful with images and photographs. We make sure there wasn't a hose sitting in the driveway or a power line in the frame. We take the time to carefully present everything we put out into the public sphere and make sure that it always delights people visually.

When refining the brand for the home you are selling, ask yourself the following questions:

- Does the brand directly relate to the home buyers you are targeting?
- Will the buyers immediately grasp it, without having to think?
- Is the brand capturing the uniqueness of the property?
- Is the message being conveyed clearly and concisely?
- Does it have a sense of authenticity, rather than sounding like an ordinary sales pitch?

Chapter 7

# BUYER BE AWARE

A young couple moved to Marin County from the Midwest knowing very little about the local real estate market. They rented a home for eight months to get a better sense of the area, but they didn't do a deep dive into home sales data. They met a local realtor, who told them she had a house coming on the market. "It hasn't been listed, but there will be a line of people who will pay $3.4 million when it comes on the market."

I had interviewed several years earlier for the same listing, but the agent who ultimately represented the home gave it a much higher valuation. I had valued it at $2,900,000, a full half-million dollars below the value she communicated to the prospective buyers.

The couple knew how scarce listings under $3.5 million were in the community. They assumed they were getting a lot of home for the money, and did not think that living on a very busy street was going to be an issue for them. They closed on the house at $3,475,000 before it was ever listed for sale on the MLS. They proceeded to spend another $300,000 performing capital improvements before they moved in.

The agent had hooked the young couple with her passing comment about the house already having a lot of interest and likely selling immediately. She created a perception of "scarcity." If buyers think a product will soon not be available to them, they're more likely to buy it. That's why a travel website like Kayak lists a price for a flight, but also includes a sidebar letting you know there are only "two more seats available at that price." The agent was inviting the buyers behind the velvet rope, giving them special access, making them feel special.

People like to feel special, but they also want to fit in. By telling them there'd be a "line of people" to buy the property, the agent also offered the couple "social proof." The agent was not completely misleading them because it was true that relatively few properties

turned over in the small town, and there would be plenty of buyers—
at the right price.

Two years later, the couple called me to list the house for sale: "We
don't really like this location. This street is too loud."

The owners were determined to recoup their money when they
listed the house. I tried to temper their expectations, explaining
that they had overpaid for the home by $500,000. Their $300,000 in
capital improvements raised the value of the home beyond the actual
expenditure, and the uptick in the market also increased it, but they
were still in the hole. The house would need to sell for $3,775,000
for them to not lose money.

A miracle buyer stepped up, and after a prolonged negotiation,
made a final offer of $3.525 million, $250,000 less than the couple's
desired number. Unfortunately, the sellers could not psychologically
adjust to the market realities and dug in their heels. The buyer
walked away, and the deal died.

The moral of the story: buyers need to do their due diligence. Treat
a home purchase with the same analytic rigor as a stock purchase or
starting a business.

Vet the property and the person who's selling it. The couple overpaid
for the home because the comps they used weren't relevant to their
street. Even though all the homes in the small town sat within a
small radius, the special characteristics of their street (busyness and
noise) created a distinct micro-economy, but the buyers had no way
of knowing that.

# THE NEIGHBORS, NOT THE NUMBERS, TELL THE STORY

Don't just look at the numbers. Walk around the neighborhood and talk to the neighbors. Knock on the doors on either side of the property: *"I'm thinking about buying a house here. Is there anything I wouldn't know from just looking at this house that you think would be important for me to know? What do you like and not like about living here? How are the neighbors? Are they welcoming? Are they tough to deal with if you want to change something in the house?"* Find out if there are any nuances in the neighborhood that are not immediately apparent.

Only by talking to the neighbors will you find out the inside story: the home one street over has a dirt track for motorcycles that whine ceaselessly every Saturday night; a man uses the sole common area in your apartment building as his virtual office; the couple in the adjacent brownstone fight incessantly; the garbage truck in the alleyway will wake your kids up at five o'clock before school on Tuesdays; or the smell at low tide is unbearable.

Neighbors can give buyers a view of the neighborhood that an agent, by law, cannot. The Civil Rights Act of 1968, commonly known as the Fair Housing Act, prevents housing discrimination based on race, religion, national origin, sex, disability, or family status. While the Act has accomplished great good, it can be frustrating for buyers when agents cannot respond to specific requests. For example, if a buyer wants to be near a synagogue or church, in a "family neighborhood" or in a "safe" area, an agent can't take those requests into consideration. Offering his or her opinion on topics where groups have protected status is a violation of the law. If a client asks, "Is this a good neighborhood for families?" an agent cannot say, "It's a great community for families." That might suggest exclusion for people who don't have children. An agent must say, "It's a great community for all types of people. I encourage you to walk around and get to know it."

Visit the building commission or go online to learn what the buildable limits are in the event you want to make changes to the home. Ask if there are regulatory constraints. A rare minnow in the adjacent creek may preclude you from expanding your home into your backyard because of environmental protection laws. Make sure there are no cell phone towers that could be problematic for your health. Ask about cell reception. If you work out of your home and you're on your cell phone all day, you'd better know the signal won't drop. If a swimming pool is of paramount importance, you have a flat lot, and you later learn that the soil on your property requires stratospherically expensive caissons for a pool, how would you feel about that?

# THE GOOD, THE BAD, AND THE UGLY

You must do a lot of your own research, but your best insurance is to rely on a professional who represents you like a son or daughter. I tell every buyer I work with, "I'm approaching the purchase as if I'm buying the house myself. I will try to talk you out of the house if I don't think it's a good investment. You can always make your own decision, but I'm going to tell you, 'Yes, I would buy the home, for these reasons.' Or, 'Please don't buy this house, for these reasons…' " It's the agent's duty to be an encyclopedia for the home, the neighborhood, and the community. Agents need to give buyers the unvarnished good, bad, and ugly on the potential purchase.

I tell my buyers that I wouldn't sell them anything that I wouldn't buy myself. Of course, we all have different priorities, but my lens examines some universals: the home as an investment, the home's potential, the location, and susceptibility to market vagaries. I don't guide people toward homes where they may not have an exit or may realize a loss down the road.

I'm overly honest with buyers. If a seller wants too much for a home and my buyer wants to overpay for that home, I send my client in writing in an email the following message: "This email notifies you that, while I understand you love the home and I will write an offer for you, my opinion is that you are paying too much based on the market comps." I do that both for the buyer's benefit and to protect myself from later being sued because the buyer regrets overpaying. I also know that there's a strong probability that I will list the property for them if they decide to sell—that's when the overpaying comes home to roost.

When buyers want to purchase a home that needs work, I tell them what they will have to put into it and how long it will take, and then I project the future value. I run comps for the buyer as if the property has already been remodeled to give them a sense of its value if the changes are made. I want to make sure they feel safe within those numbers.

## You Never Know What Sits Beneath the Surface: The Value of a Home Inspection

We've talked about the home inspection from the seller's perspective; now, let's look at the buyer's. A home inspection is one of the most important steps in the home buying process, and not a place to cut corners. Knowing the condition of a home gives a buyer peace of mind. A home inspection is an objective visual examination of the physical structure and systems of a house by a third party. The standard home inspector's report covers the condition of the home's heating system, central air conditioning system, interior plumbing and electrical systems, the roof, the attic, visible insulation, walls, ceilings, floors, windows, doors, foundation, basement, and structural components.[48]

While an inspection will provide a snapshot of a house's overall condition, it might not reveal hidden problems such as pests, mold, or asbestos, or reveal defects in areas outside the inspector's purview. It also won't turn up flaws in areas that are below ground or otherwise inaccessible to the inspector, like wells and septic tanks. Depending on the characteristics of the house, the following additional inspections may be required:

- Pest Inspection
- Drainage Inspection
- Tree/Arborist Inspection
- Structural Inspection
- Chimney Inspection

- Pool/Spa Inspection
- Mold Inspection
- Well Inspection

Accompany the inspector when he or she examines the home. You will have a better grasp of the issues of the home and you will learn how to maintain your home going forward.

If a seller gives a buyer a pre-inspection report, should it be taken at face value? Only if the seller's inspection reports were done by the best inspector in the county, and done recently. If the inspection report is not recent, at a bare minimum, engage your own inspector and walk through the house to examine and verify the findings of the original report.

# **❙ YABBA DABBA DON'T**

People get stuck when they build to their specific predilections with no thought of resale. The monolithic dome structure might appeal to fans of *The Flintstones*, the iconic 1960s television series, but the buyer pool will be limited to Stone Age families when it hits the market.

I encourage people who are considering buying or building a home with an unconventional layout to look down the road. If they are buying solely for the experience of living in the home and are not concerned about building or retaining value, that should be acknowledged up front. For those who want to buy a home with an unconventional layout *and* monetize that investment, those desires are often at odds, and the buyer should be forewarned by their representative. I tell my clients, for example, "You need to understand that it's going to be challenging in a school-driven market to have the kids' bedrooms two floors below. I don't care if there's an intercom system, it's a psychological issue for buyers."

# THE TITANIC WAS "UNSINKABLE": PREPARE FOR THE UNEXPECTED

Optimism, the belief that that the future will work out, is a healthy psychological framework, but life doesn't simply reward us for positive thinking. Homeowners need to be prepared for the unexpected before purchasing and occupying a residence. Exogenous events or personal life-changing experiences like divorce, job loss, work relocation, or health problems can quickly alter a homeowner's financial landscape.

Combining such an event with a market downturn can pose a real hardship, particularly for owners who are overly leveraged or didn't have much equity in their homes. You don't want to go to market when your asset has lost 20 or 30 percent overnight, but people with insufficient cash reserves and income, who can no longer make the mortgage or debt payments, may not have a choice.

Even in the best of markets, sellers divesting a home to relieve economic hardship in most cases leave money on the table. These homeowners often also forego preparing their home for the market because they don't have the money to update it. In the worst cases in any market, lenders take back the keys and foreclose on the home.

I recommend owners retain a minimum of twenty-four months of mortgage payments in the bank to get them through difficult times—or else don't purchase the home. Too often homeowners find themselves in a position where they can't afford their home any longer. Homeowners need to be adaptable and prepared if material circumstances change. Leasing the home could be one possibility, depending on the strength of the rental market, which is also subject to market forces. Planning for a rough patch is imperative.

## Going Down with the Titanic

The emotive component of real estate causes people to hang onto their homes when they should let go. This was prevalent in 2008–10, when the country's wealthiest communities and poorest areas saw waves of short sales and foreclosures. From 2001 through 2007, our economy was in a cycle of prosperity. People were building mega-homes that were severely leveraged. When the housing markets crashed, many homeowners who couldn't afford to ride out the housing market until it picked up again in 2013 went down with their homes.

During this time, people would call me and say, "I haven't made my payments in months and I need to sell my house." Had they called me before they stopped making payments, they could have sold their house for more, saved their credit and, in some cases, avoided foreclosure.

So why do homeowners go down with the Titanic? It's not just that we have an emotional attachment to homes, though that surely plays a part. The answer might lie in our relationship with loss. In a 1979 study, psychologists Kahenman and Tversky demonstrated that "losses loom larger than gains."[49] They discovered that we feel the pain of loss much more intensely than we feel the pleasure of an equivalent gain. Imagine a coin toss where you had to give someone ten dollars if it landed on heads, but you would receive fourteen dollars if it came up tails. Surely, a rational person would take that deal, right? Nope. They found most people had to be able to win almost twice the amount they could lose before they would accept the bet. We avoid the pain of loss at all costs. Those homeowners would rather risk losing more money than come to terms with the immediate perceived loss. They will stay on the Titanic until the top deck starts to slip under water, rather than getting on a lifeboat when the bells sound.

# ▍YOUR HOME IS NOT AN ATM

A man walks up to a window in the front of a house, slides a card out of his wallet, and slips the card into a narrow horizontal slot. He looks around to make sure that no one's watching, punches a four-letter code into the adjacent keypad, withdraws the card, makes a selection, and reaches forward in response to a computer-generated whirring sound.

A thief? A repairman fine-tuning a high-tech security system? No. A homeowner withdrawing money from his house.

It's not science fiction. The modern American home has evolved, for many, into a cash dispenser. An ATM.

Rapidly rising property values across America have been the primary driver for increased equity in homes. Home equity is the appraised value of a home minus any mortgage debt on the home. It's a common practice for people to borrow against a home's available equity, or "take equity out" of the house. Homeowners have a few options to get cash out of their homes.

Let's say, for example, your home is worth $400,000 and you have a $200,000 mortgage on it. You have $200,000 of equity, or 50 percent of the value of the home. You want to take $100,000 out of the home. Most lenders require that homeowners have, at a minimum, 20 percent equity in their homes, so that there's a cushion if the market tumbles.

**Home value:** $400,000

**Existing mortgage:** $200,000 (current loan balance)

**Initial home equity:** $200,000

**Cash withdrawn:** $100,000

**Remaining home equity:** $100,000 (25 percent)

With a "cash-out refinance," borrowers pay off the existing mortgage, take out a larger mortgage, and put the cash difference in their pockets. The cash can then be used for whatever purposes the borrower chooses.

**Home value:** $400,000

**Existing mortgage:** $200,000 (current loan balance)

**Initial home equity:** $200,000

**Cash-out refinance:** $300,000 (new loan balance)

**Cash withdrawn:** $100,000

**Remaining home equity:** $100,000 (25 percent)

The new mortgage increases by $100,000. The owner pockets $100,000 and has $100,000 less equity in the home.

Another option is that a homeowner can take out a home equity loan. It's a lump sum loan that uses the home as collateral. The $100,000 loan, also known as a second mortgage, raises the existing liens by $100,000, lowers the equity by $100,000, and puts $100,000 in the hands of the owner.

**Home value:** $400,000

**Existing mortgage:** $200,000 (current loan balance)

**Initial home equity:** $200,000

**New mortgages: $200,000** (1st mortgage) **+ $100,000** (2nd mortgage)

**Cash withdrawn:** $100,000

**Remaining home equity:** $100,000 (25 percent)

An alternative to the home equity loan is a home equity line of credit (HELOC). Also secured by the home, a HELOC is a revolving line of credit that allows you to borrow up to a certain amount, rather than receiving a fixed dollar amount. Unlike a fixed home equity loan, the interest rate is variable, generally tied to an index like the prime rate.

People often think taking equity out of their home is a way of putting their money to work but, in reality, they are acquiring more debt. Until a house sells, equity is an unrealized and fluctuating estimate of value. If home prices plummet, the value of the home could overnight be less than the mortgage. I witnessed this scenario over and over in the financial crisis of 2008.

Too many homeowners were pulling cash out of their homes, not to make other investments or capital improvements, but to support their lifestyles. They kept pushing the ATM buttons until the market leveled them.

Then, instead of cutting their losses, they held on for dear life, careening down with the market until the bank pulled the plug.

Chapter 8

# DIDN'T AUNT LOUISE JUST GET LICENSED? FINDING THE RIGHT AGENT

> *"Trust and integrity are precious resources, easily squandered, hard to regain."*
>
> **–Sissela Bok**

The agent you select to manage the acquisition or sale of your home is the first, and maybe the most important, decision you'll make. For most of us, real estate deals are the largest financial transactions of our lives, and there's no room for mistakes. But all too often, we passively engage the person who's going to represent us. Unaware of the importance of the agent's role, social or familial obligation often controls sellers' selection. Buying or selling a home is not the time to throw a bone to your friend who moonlights as a real estate agent, or your relative who recently got his real estate license and lives a hundred miles down the interstate.

## DRIVING AWAY WITH TEARS IN MY EYES

I represented a home in a housing development in a quiet, wooded valley in Marin County, close to director George Lucas's famed Skywalker Ranch. Homes rarely come on the market in the small enclave. Surprisingly, a property down the street was put up for sale a week after our listing. Ours sold with multiple offers, but the other property did not move and was eventually taken off the market.

Five months later, after the market started to turn down, the owner of the unsold home called. "We want to hire you, based on what some friends from the neighborhood have told us about you. Can you meet with us?"

When the market starts shifting down, and homes aren't selling to people's expectations, buyers get more discerning about who they hire. In an up market that's trading fast and furious, people don't feel much due diligence is required. They are confident they can sell their home without much effort. When they start to hear news snippets about the market softening or prices falling, they do their homework and go to the top people. A flight to quality.

After we hung up, I clicked on their previous MLS listing. The marketing for the home had been terrible. The online photographs took prospective buyers inside the house, outside, back inside, and then finished on a shot of the barren dirt side yard. The bathrooms were completely left out of the photos.

The owners, a warm, engaging couple, greeted me at the door with a hug. "We already knew we were hiring you, so there's a key under the mat for you." They were both attorneys. He represented inmates who had been wrongfully imprisoned, and his wife operated a legal clinic for low-income individuals and families. "We don't make that much money. Most of what we've earned has gone into our children's education. We are putting our son through law school. We are tapped out financially and want to move on from this home." Their nest was empty, and they wanted to move into a smaller home in the state where their son was in school.

They had all the reports and disclosures laid out on the counter, buttoned-up and organized. She said, "Here's everything you need. We'll do anything you say. We'll move out of here, if necessary." They were ready to grab their suitcases and walk out the door. "We just don't want to be here anymore. All the bedrooms are empty. The kids are gone."

When people are emotionally ready to move on and they've been worn down by the sales process, they often want to just give up. All the energy they had at the beginning of the process dissipates.

A Ralph Lauren sofa with big floral patterns straight out of the 1991 catalog anchored the living room. Tapestry art from Costco adorned the walls. Oriental rugs were scattered throughout the house. "Tracy, we were told we didn't need to stage our home, and we made substantial improvements, but there was no response from buyers. We think we made a huge mistake hiring our agent."

They had spent $240,000 getting their home into shape, including $45,000 on membrane roofing and $8,000 on a spa tub that they dropped into old tile from the original construction of the home. Instead of restaining the dated blond, thin-cut oak hardwood floors, they put high-gloss finish on them. They repainted the entire interior the same pale blue color it had always been. They replaced the lighting with heavy sconces that lined the hallways.

I was direct. "I'm sorry to tell you this, but you are never going to get the full financial return on most of these expenditures, and you'll get a zero return on some of them because a lot of this stuff has to come out. Buyers might appreciate having a high-end roof, but they don't value it on a dollar-to-dollar basis. People don't want spa tubs, and putting a new appliance in the old tub deck only highlights the age of the bathrooms. The house needs to be repainted. The lighting has to be replaced. And the floors need to be refinished."

I left their house with tears in my eyes. The couple couldn't have been any nicer—kind people doing good for the community. They were organized and diligent in preparing their home for market, but they made one costly mistake. They hired an agent who didn't have a clue about maximizing value in a home. He ticked the right boxes, staging and updating, but he didn't have the slightest understanding of design, market demand, and how to guide them through that process. The couple may as well have installed a wood-burning stove, stuffed it with money, and lit it with a match, because most of their initial investment went up in smoke.

# VCRS, PAY PHONES, REAL ESTATE AGENTS?

Many industry observers hypothesize that technology is driving real estate agents into obsolescence. Just as Expedia, Orbitz, and Kayak have rendered travel agents obsolete, and Amazon has wiped out the brick-and-mortar booksellers, does the Information Age portend the extinction of agents who buy and sell homes? Many people believe that an agent's primary asset—knowledge—can be better sourced through unbiased, publicly available data, packaged and served up for free on platforms like Trulia, Zillow, or Redfin.

The wealth management business offers a more relevant reference for the future of real estate agents than the industries that have disappeared. Individual investors have almost as much access to information as professional traders. The abundance of trading platforms and free technologies and services make it easier than ever for individuals to trade securities. They can manage their own portfolios for free. In theory, financial advisors should be relics of the past. But they are not. According to Forbes, financial advisor is the third most in-demand job in 2018. Why? Because there's a wide chasm between having information and being an expert.

Similarly, while technological transformation is making the real estate market radically more efficient and accessible, a computer cannot explain why a home purchase will go up or down in value, why it may flatline, when to fix it up, how to fix it up, how to best position it in the marketplace, or whether to invest in it at all. Machine intelligence cannot respond in real time to the myriad of complex, challenging emotional and psychological issues that arise during the course of a real estate listing and transaction.

So far, consumers seem to agree. More than half of buyers found the home they purchased on the internet, but at the same time, 87 percent of buyers purchased their home through a real estate agent or broker, according to the National Association of Realtors' 2017 Profile of Home Buyers and Sellers.

I'm not a blind advocate for real estate agents. As we've touched on, the industry is littered with opportunists who give the rest a bad name. But an agent can bring tremendous value to the sale or purchase of a home. I'm going to help you identify what makes a great agent.

# ▋ DO DUE DILIGENCE

*"This is about your commission…"*

*"I have a house I want you to represent, but it's probably not big enough for you…"*

*"I know this is going to be a low priority because the house is only worth one million."*

If I had a dollar for every time I've heard one of these comments, I'd retire to Aspen and write a book about real estate. I'm not driven by commissions. The size of the sale doesn't matter. I work to support my family, but I'm driven by a purpose, not a paycheck. I find meaning in what I do, a connection to larger community. I derive satisfaction from helping people find a new home or sell their existing home—and doing something well.

Popular culture has a narrow view of commission-based sales positions that reduces motivation down to a single financial carrot. In my experience, successful people in any field are often driven by larger forces—the desire to participate in or accomplish something that's bigger than themselves, to be of service, or to advance their skill set in a vocation that matters. Whether you are collecting bridge tolls or designing robotics, people who find meaning in what they do outperform those who care only about the paycheck.

In his book *Drive*, motivation expert Daniel Pink cites evidence to support the idea that intrinsic motivation matters more than extrinsic motivators. In the mid-1990s, Microsoft started a digital encyclopedia called Encarta. They paid professional editors, researchers, and managers to oversee the massive project and delivered it several years later. In 2001, Jimmy Wales and Larry Sanger launched a similar idea, except their version was a publicly editable encyclopedia where people would contribute for fun and no contributor would get paid a cent. It seemed obvious at the time who'd win that battle between competing ideas.

Wales and Sanger were bringing a water gun to a knife fight. Nobody could have predicted that fifteen years later their brainchild, Wikipedia, would be the fifth largest website in the world, but it speaks to the idea that people want to be a part of something that matters. Some other sources of motivation that explain why people do what they do are creativity, challenge, acknowledgement, identity, and pride.

The notion that people are driven by greater motivations than money also holds true in the real estate business.

For best results, choose from among agents who love what they do, who are intrinsically motivated by the meaningfulness of their work, who place the client's interest ahead of their own. Agents' overriding mission must be to provide their client with the unadulterated truth, even if they risk losing the business. Agents don't have that freedom if their singular motivation is cashing a check. This may sound idealistic or naïve, especially coming from an agent, but it's the truth.

I recently represented a house in an upscale suburban neighborhood that was getting a paltry response. The market had dropped since it was listed three months earlier. We had a single offer and one showing. I wrote the sellers a long, blunt email.

Dear Andrew and Josie,

I hope it's okay to be somewhat candid with you. At the end of the day, I would rather be very honest with you as clients, so that you may make the best decision going forward for you and your family. We initially met in early winter on the heels of the sale in [your town] that closed $200,000 over the list price, $625 per square foot. The house had been previously fully renovated with about $100,000 in recent capital improvements to get it ready for the market. At that time, I felt that adjusting your home to $605 per square foot was appropriate. However, that was approximately three months ago and there has been a market change since that time. I spoke with three of my colleagues and they concur that the market has flattened in your community. Traditionally, [your town] is a second-choice market for buyers who typically prefer other parts of Marin that have stronger school districts.

When markets shift, markets like [your town] are the first markets to experience the change. I have three active listings in [your town] right now, and I am experiencing this issue on all three. There is no doubt in my mind that the market is shifting down.

We have had only a single buyer ask to see your house. The listing is very well publicized and on approximately fifteen websites with hundreds of hits and no other requests for showings. That tells me that the house is overpriced for the current market. In twenty years of selling homes, I have not had this happen. Fortunately, we have an offer on the table from the only party that has asked to see it. These buyers are willing to absorb the cost of a new roof, any sewer lateral work that is outstanding and go through the retroactive permitting process. I am concerned that if you do not accept this offer, we will be selling the house at a far lower price point weeks or months down the road. If you feel that renting your home is a better alternative for you, I entirely support that option. I believe there would be plenty of people who would love to lease your home. I want the very best for you and your family.

Tracy

My clients called immediately and thanked me. My email made them understand that they were my top priority, not the commission from the sale of the home, and that I really was giving them my best advice. They decided to rent their home and sold it three years later when the market was stronger.

Agents who don't disconnect from the commission, who are afraid of losing the business, soft-pedal the truth during every step of the process. Let's say an agent goes into a home and knows that changing some design elements will lead to a higher sale price. The seller resists staging or doing anything to the home. Instead of pushing back and risking discord, the agent acquiesces, even though he knows it will cost the seller a lot of money. Or imagine an agent knows the return on investment will be higher on property A than property B, even though the latter property might have more immediate appeal to the buyer. An agent who's working for himself rather than the buyer won't try to direct the buyer toward a different choice for fear of alienating the buyer and losing the commission. He will subordinate his expertise, and therefore maximizing value for the client, to the client's perceived desires or demands. In doing so, he's abnegating his paramount purpose in the transaction— to advocate for the client's best interests even if it places the engagement at risk.

# References

So how do you make sure you're making a good choice? Start by calling an agent's references. It's basic, but very important. Try to find references from clients whose buying or selling needs are similar to yours. Ask questions:

1. How did the sale or purchase price get established?

2. How quickly did the home sell, and do the sellers think their home was in alignment with market value?

3. Did the seller feel that the agent always acted in the client's best interests?

4. Was the agent responsive?

5. What was the range of services the agent provided to you?

6. Would you work with the agent again?

7. How did the sellers feel about the agent's negotiation capabilities?

8. How broad and innovative was the agent's marketing?

9. How well did the agent vet the buyers' financial qualifications?

10. How much time and effort did the agent expend preparing your house for the market?

11. Was the agent's team organized?

12. Was the agent communicative throughout the process?

13. The answers will flush out agents who are incompetent or unethical.

## The Truth Lies in the Numbers

Most people click on a website and see pretty photos and an agent's marketing campaign, but rarely dig deeper. That's fine if you are hiring the agent's web designer, but to really find out about your agent, look at the data. Agents should provide you with statistics that reflect their expertise and ability to sell your home.

Check how many of the agent's listings were withdrawn, taken off the market, or canceled. A withdrawn listing means the property is still listed with a broker or agent, but is no longer on the Multiple

Listing Service (MLS). Taken off the market means the contract between the client and agent came to an end on an expired listing. When the seller and agent mutually agreed to terminate the listing, it is canceled.

Look at agents' sales history. Have they consistently been closing the same number of homes each year? Is their business growing every year? What is their record of performance in a softer economy? A lot of agents can transact during "up" markets, but an up market can often last only three to four years. How does the agent perform in a down or soft market? Perhaps most important, look at agents' percentage of original list price to eventual sale price. If it is above 95 percent, they are doing their job right. If it is below that, you want to cross them off the list.

The metric of original list price to closed sales price percentage reflects the difference between the two prices. My average every year is 99 to 99.5 percent.

Obligation, social commitment, familial relationship, and guilt should play no part in agent selection. Choosing a real estate agent should be done with the same care as hiring a lawyer or financial advisor. Hire only the best.

# ❙ GO LOCAL

I bought a home outside the market where I'm an expert without using a local agent—and paid the price. I purchased a property in St. Helena, on the floor of the Napa Valley. The town is only sixty miles north of where I live, but it has its own local knowledge. I ran the numbers for comparable properties. I looked at new construction. What I didn't know is that properties two miles north of the town of St. Helena, where the home was located, are worth significantly less than properties south of the town. Traffic congestion has impacted the valley floor, making it a nightmare for people from San Francisco to return from their weekend homes or travel to the northern parts of the Valley. People will pay much more to live in Rutherford, Yountville, and Oakville, the towns south of St. Helena. I grossly overpaid for the home. I made a mistake by not having a professional represent me. Nuances and trends exist in every market that you can't know unless you are in that market all day every day.

A lot of people ask if I'll represent them in Silicon Valley, which is an hour south of Marin County. I tell them that I'll find them a great local representative, but I can't accept the engagement. I don't eat, breathe, and live there.

I have a friend who represents properties in four markets. While I appreciate her hustle, her priority is money, not her clients. Real estate agents can represent anyone, anywhere in the state where they are licensed, but that doesn't mean they can do it effectively.

# I HOPE THE FRIENDSHIP WAS WORTH HALF A MILLION DOLLARS

A homeowner named Jane, a sixty-year-old woman in a wealthy suburb in Marin County with kids in college, had recently gone through a divorce. She had not worked for years and did not have an income of her own. At the time of separation, Jane and her husband agreed that she would take title to the family house, with the understanding that proceeds from the sale would support her for the remainder of her life.

If the right agent had been hired, the house would have been appropriately appraised at approximately $5.2 million. It was a beautiful property, but the layout of the house was confusing. The dining room was enormous and there was no family room. An awkward transition connected the downstairs to the outside pool area.

Jane gave the listing to a newly licensed New York socialite who had been a great sounding board throughout her divorce. The agent had little experience selling homes and absolutely no experience selling $5 million homes.

The agent's choice in room staging highlighted the problems of the house rather than fixing them. Instead of staging the large space off the kitchen as a family room, she presented it as a dining room. She set up a small nook off the dining room as the family room, effectively reminding buyers that there was no family room. The right staging could have remedied the clunky passage to the pool area by guiding people to a different egress, but she didn't do it. The color palette of the home was out of date and adversely impacted the photos and the marketing of the home.

As the coup de grace, the agent overpriced the home at $5.6 million, $400,000 more than it was worth.

A few weeks after the property came on the market, I brought some clients to look at it. We made an offer at $5.2 million and the agent chose not to respond to our offer. The deal died. My client bought another home. After six weeks, the price dropped to $5.3 million. The house sat for three months and the price dropped to $4.9 million. They briefly took the home off the market and restaged it with the stager they should have used at the outset.

Six months later, I went back with new clients and we paid $4.568 million for the house. The agent's failure to properly represent the home cost Jane more than half a million dollars, not including the staging and carrying costs. Two staging attempts ($40,000), two paints jobs ($20,000), six months of mortgage carrying costs ($36,000), and the rental that she occupied during the sale of her home ($30,000) were additional costs resulting from the agent's poor choices. Afterward, I told Jane's ex-husband, "I hope that relationship is worth half a million dollars, because that's what her choice of representation cost her."

Jane didn't know about all the bad decisions that were made along the way because she didn't know enough to know. She thought that was all her house was worth. It was worth much more than $4.6 million.

Ironically, a few months later, Bill, another seller on the same street, called me. His house had been on the market with another agent for a protracted period of time with multiple price drops. The marketing was wrong, and the price kept falling. He wanted my advice. I explained why the home wasn't selling and where the price needed to be. Bill said, "I can't believe I hired this woman." When I asked him about the relationship, Bill told me she had sold his family their first home. For years afterward, she ingratiated herself with the family. If they were leaving for a vacation, she picked them up and drove them to the airport. She was like their limousine driver, Bill said. When it came time to sell the house, they felt obligated to use her.

Bill's house undersold by several hundred thousand dollars. With that money, Bill could have bought a limousine and hired a full-time driver. An expensive ride to the airport.

# ▌ BUYING A LISTING

You decide to sell your home and begin interviewing real estate agents. You've done your homework. You know what's on the market, what has recently sold, and the sale prices. You also know what makes your house different, unique, and you communicate your feelings to the prospective agents. The agents give you market data, comps, and valuations—and make a case for why they are best suited to represent your home. One agent, though, really seems to get your property. It's like meeting someone at a party who looks directly in your eyes and says, "You're special." This agent wants to list your house at a price far above the others. You're overwhelmed with euphoria and relief that someone finally sees the light. The words are wonderfully reassuring, validating.

In your excitement and desire to cash in on your home, you ignore all the other data and sign a listing agreement with Mr. Right. Unfortunately, you have just fallen for an all too common and unethical practice known as "buying a listing." The agent has given you an inflated sales price to get your business, knowing the house won't sell with that bloated price tag.

So why does the agent take on the listing? Like any business, activity in real estate hints at success. A "For Sale" sign is a billboard for an agent. Fielding calls and holding open houses puts the agent in the midst of buyers looking for homes. He or she can "flip" them and show them other properties in their price range.

The practice is more common with new agents whose focus is to build a book of business. The catch-22 is that they cannot get listings if they don't have listings, so they'll subordinate the truth or transparency for their career. Desperate to legitimize themselves by getting sales under their belts, they tell prospective clients what they want to hear, rather than what they should hear. The agent rides it out until the seller agrees to reduce the price, even though the strategy risks bleeding the agent financially—it costs money to represent and market a home.

An agent complained to me that she spent $25,000 on a rock star's listing and it wasn't moving. Her comment was intended to engender sympathy, as if she were the victim of an unpredictable market. In fact, she had significantly overvalued the house to get the listing, but she didn't mention that important piece of information. Months later, after chasing the market down with several price drops, the house sold for far less that it was worth.

This type of deception is all too common in real estate. It's harder to detect than outright lying, but the consequences for the client are profound. False information undermines owners' ability to make rational decisions in their own best interest.

# A PUNCH LIST: QUESTIONS TO ASK A PROSPECTIVE AGENT

## Buyer's Agent

- What's your philosophy to find me the best house?
- What makes you good at what you do?
- Are you able to discern which homes are better investments?
- Will you tell me if a home I like is not a good investment?
- Will you tell me something I don't want to hear?
- If I decide to buy something and it needs capital improvements, will you be able to guide me through it, e.g., provide design input in accordance with the tastes of the market?
- How will you negotiate if there's more than one offer? How will I know that I'm getting the house without overpaying?
- Will you tell me if you think an overbid is a bad investment?
- Can you help me find a lender?
- Will you help me personalize an offer if there are multiple bids so I have the best chance of getting the home?
- How do you make sure I don't lose a house if there are multiple offers?
- How do you manage my time so I'm not looking at homes I don't want?
- Do you have a bias toward certain locations?

# Seller's Agent

- Can I see your sales statistics in the MLS for the past five years?

- How many sales listings have you had in the past five years, as opposed to buyer representations? Can I see your average list to sales price percentage?

- How are you going to price my home?

- What suggestions do you have to get it ready for the market?

- How are you going to brand and market my home?

- How will that marketing be differentiated from other agents' marketing?

- How will you communicate with prospective buyers?

- How will you encourage a buyer to increase their offer if they don't want to pay the list price?

- How will you update and communicate with us about interest in our home?

- Will you send a weekly marketing update?

- What will your negotiations look like?

- Do you handle the direction of marketing for the home, including the word choice and descriptive language, the imagery, the sequencing of the imagery, the story behind the house—or is that delegated to an assistant?

# Chapter 9

# BUYING AND SELLING HOMES: WHAT THE FUTURE LOOKS LIKE

R eal estate is the largest commodity in the global economy. With an estimated $217 trillion in assets, the value of real estate is four times larger than all the public companies in the world, according to a report by the real estate company Savillis.[50] Residential property accounts for 75 percent of the global value of property. It's too big to escape major disruptive influences, and big changes are coming.

Technological innovation has already levied its impact on residential real estate. The first phase of innovation was driven by companies like Zillow, Trulia, and Redfin, aggregators who provide information on homes listed for sale on the MLS (and others) directly to consumers. The MLS gave permissions to these real estate sites to republish the listing feeds on their media channels. Before the arrival of the aggregators, home buyers and sellers had very minimal access to listings. The information was only available to agents and brokers and zealously monopolized by traditional real estate brokerages who feared irrelevance if the public had access inside the castle walls. Maximizing the exposure of listings on the high-traffic national aggregator sites is now a fixture in most home sales marketing plans.

The aggregators, and their focus on data transparency, democratized access to information. A more informed consumer can now navigate the labyrinth of residential real estate. But so far, they have not disrupted the traditional model. The essential sales process has not yet been fundamentally transformed.

How do we know a transformation is coming? A few factors point to it.

## ▎ MONEY TALKS

In 2017, more than $5 billion in venture capital poured into real estate technology companies, compared to $33 million invested in 2010. Technology-driven investors, after success transforming traditional businesses like taxis and hotels, have set their sights on the antiquated real estate business model. It's inevitable that this kind of capital will make some waves.

# ARTIFICIAL INTELLIGENCE

The infusion of money heralds significant reform, and the technology exists to drive it. The advent and exponentially increasing sophistication of artificial intelligence enables machines to perform sophisticated "human" tasks like judgment and evaluation, problem-solving, pattern recognition, and decision-making. The technology is only getting better, and the possible applications to the real estate industry are limitless. Programs will be able to crunch thousands of data points to highlight potential buyers and target them with digital ads. Properties will be matched to people based on personal preferences and personality traits. Real estate platforms won't just display more information to provide value; their value will come from providing information that's directly relevant to the person looking for a home. Machine learning algorithms will be able to identify real estate investment opportunities.

# THE MILLENNIAL MINDSET

Finally, and perhaps most importantly, consumers will demand change. The next wave of real estate's disruption will be propelled by and for millennials, also called Gen Y, the generation born between 1980 and 1997. Millennials make up 27 percent of the earth's population,[51] the largest generational group in history. According to a study by UNC's Kenan-Flagler Business School, millennials will comprise 46 percent of the US workforce by 2020.[52] Millennials are moving into the peak of their spending years and represent 34 percent of all home buyers.[53] Each generation has distinguishing characteristics, and millennials are no different.

Millennials are connected and collaborative. They have grown up in a world with unfettered access to information: Google, Wikipedia, TED, YouTube, and blogs, conversations fueled by the masses. Their learning style relies on collective knowledge shared digitally, as reflected in crowdsourcing, Yelp reviews, and a reliance on peer groups and social media. They resist business structures where information is siloed off with one person.

Millennials value efficiency. They would rather instant-message their department head than walk down to the corner office. The idea of sending multiple emails on a group chain, booking a meeting room, sending invites, walking to a conference room, or having a discussion doesn't make sense to millennials. They prefer to post their business development report to a shared area.

Millennials also value customization. Customization is the future of many industries, including medicine. Increasingly, society is understanding and capitalizing on the fact that one size does not fit all. Millennials and younger generations have an expectation of customized experiences and transactions, and these preferences are driving evolution in every industry, not just real estate.

In short, millennials have an expectation of an efficient, fluid, seamless, customized user experience that allows them to accomplish their goals. Their value system is antithetical to the old-world, inefficient, compartmentalized, and technologically deficient nature of both real estate transactions and traditional brokerages.

## Reinventing the Sales Process

The sales process itself will evolve, becoming less expensive, less stressful, and faster for buyers and sellers.

Robert Refkin, the CEO of Compass, is one of the millennials leading the charge. He observes: "The basic process for selling homes hasn't changed in 75 years. The industry is at a Blockbusters-Netflix crossroads. The traditional model is radically inefficient."

The inefficient, opaque, and nerve-grating buying and selling experience consumes its participants. In the course of a single transaction, buyers and sellers work with real estate agents, brokerages, appraisers, loan officers, mortgage lenders, home inspectors, title companies, accountants, lawyers, contractors, stagers, and photographers—all while trying to keep their day jobs and raise their families.

The workflow of residential real estate is archaic. Buyers and sellers engage in tedious, inefficient activities performed on multiple platforms. The agent conducts the symphony of moving components, but the onus still falls on the client to navigate among them. Rather than a smart phone, imagine if you had one device for maps and navigation, another device for photos, a device that records memos, a device for emailing, a device to play music, a device to check Facebook, a device that forecasts the weather, a device to search the internet, and a device to call home. That would impede productivity, and it's not unlike the Byzantine, fragmented workflow of residential real estate sales.

Collaborative software can allow all parties in a real estate transaction to work toward the same goal expediently and efficiently. We have the technology—along with the expectation that technology will drive all experiences—to bring efficiency to the long-standing and old-fashioned system of transacting homeownership. This same software will also bring the coveted customization millennials crave.

The ultimate benefit? Faster, streamlined, customized transactions will translate to less anxiety. Surveys show that buying and selling homes is one of the most stressful events in modern life.[54] A British poll revealed that buying a house is more taxing than divorce, bankruptcy, and even the death of a loved one. (That was a joke.)

# THE TRADITIONAL BROKERAGE– CALLING A TAXI TO TAKE YOU TO BLOCKBUSTER

Transforming the sales process requires transforming the traditional brokerage. Brokerages that resist technological change risk facing obsolescence.

For decades, residential real estate brokerages have enjoyed enormous profits while providing a poor customer experience and little value, simply because consumers lacked options. As a result, the traditional brokerage now has a target on its back.

The traditional brokerage struggles to add value to the real estate transaction. By law, real estate agents must work under a broker's license. The brokerage provides oversight, consultation, and legal support to ensure that transactions get executed properly in exchange for a sizable percentage of the agent's commission.

Historically, the brokerage provided an agent an office and desk, a letterhead, legal support, marketing materials, continuing education seminars, tools for building a career, and leads to generate business. Equal to the support they provided, their value lay in their brand presence. Customers had confidence that large brokerage brands would ensure maximum exposure for their homes.

Refkin identifies the flawed foundation upon which the broker-agent relationship is established: "Brokers have operated under two, almost paternal, misconceptions. First, brokerages act as if agents are salespeople. In fact, they are business owners. Second, brokerages have cultivated the perception that agents are employees that need to be managed. They are not employees. Agents are customers of the brokerage. Years ago, brokerage firms somehow convinced agents not to sell themselves but sell the company. But it's almost like a landlord-tenant relationship with a logo. Brokerages are not companies in the traditional sense."

The mammoth shift to digital marketing, social media, and real estate marketplaces has dramatically reduced the value of traditional brokerages. Agents fulfill many of the roles that were once performed by brokerages. The expensive ads that a brokerage took out in newspapers and magazines no longer matter because print advertising is dead in real estate, supplanted by digital marketing. Agents market at their own cost. Mentoring and training is of little value to established agents. Newer agents have access to endless online training materials. The best mentoring for a new agent is to work for an established agent. A brokerage's brand presence means little to customers. According to data from the National Association of Realtors, only about 3 percent of buyers and 4 percent of sellers consider an agent's association with a firm to be an important factor in hiring that agent.

The truth is that agents are the brand, not the brokerages where they hang their shingle. An agent's competitive advantage is their name and client base.

# ▎THE BROKERAGE OF THE FUTURE

The brokerage of the future will be a single integrated real estate services platform that provides technology tools to the stakeholders—agents, buyers, and sellers—facilitating seamless collaboration on all steps of the home buying process. Agents in brokerages will have a workflow that encompasses the whole transaction, not just a slice of it. For the first time, all the constituents of the sales process will exist together in one place.

- Agents will have access to all deal elements on one screen at the push of a button, to track everything from listing appointments, real-time market data, and valuations to the update on your loan application, instead of using on average eleven different software programs per day (out of more than three hundred products available to the market).

- An agent's marketing—brochures, digital marketing, social media, and paid social media—will all be accessible through the platform. Presently, an agent must go to three different companies to add photos to a brochure, social media, and digital marketing. Three different logins. Three times uploading the photos.

- The concierge service providers that some agents offer will likely be accessible on the platform. Home buyers are the portal for many other expensive purchases: move-in services, mortgages, title and escrow, painters, stagers, roofers, inspectors, contractors, architects, and interior designers.

Real Estate Rescue

Rather than the agent being the repository for the information and contacts, it'll be shared and four-star-rated.

- Blockchain will expedite the escrow and mortgage processes, as government regulations adapt to fit the needs of the digital economy. The authorized participants in the process will be able to check the status of a mortgage approval, review the bank's appraisal, examine the title report, and click on a ledger to track land ownership, minimizing paperwork and expediting closing.

- Big data on the platform will empower buyers, sellers, and agents with insights to make better decisions. Complex learning algorithms enabling machines to grow smarter over time will be harnessed for a range of purposes. Long-term values of properties will be predicted. Marketing will be targeted to buyers who fit profiles. Valuations will improve. Computers will offer opinions that were once the sole domain of agents. Pattern recognition will highlight homes or areas that are undervalued.

Brokerages will separate into two camps: one of technology-driven companies where agents will remain central in the transaction and offer a more integrated and seamless experience for buyers and sellers, and another consisting of value-focused platforms that enable buyers and sellers to transact directly without an agent driving the process.

Agents will continue to play a substantive role in heterogeneous markets, particularly the higher-end markets, where differentiated product creates a barrier to entry for machine learning. The need for human voices, local expertise, personal relationships, and refined negotiating skills; the complexity of transactions; questions of timing in the marketplace; and many other factors will continue to create demand for well-intentioned, honest, and experienced agents. For twenty years, I've watched scenarios unfold that even the best Hollywood producers could not script—along with problems that the most sophisticated machines can't solve.

- You are going to be closing escrow on Thursday. The night before escrow closing (right before you go on record), torrential rainstorms hit, the roof leaks, and waters pours in and warps the hardwood floors. A water remediation company is brought in. Can a "machine" get the buyer and seller through that scenario and save the deal?

- You find the home of your dreams when you were not even looking. You decide, one week before Thanksgiving, to sell your home to buy the new house. Is a machine going to pull your home together in a matter of days and prepare it with the right furniture, paint colors, accessories, pricing advice, and marketing strategy, and then manage multiple offers on it so that you can quickly purchase the home of your dreams? Oh, and by the way, that machine will never be able to convince the owner of the home you are purchasing that your home will sell quickly enough.

- A divorcing couple's home is set to close. The day before closing, the husband is served with a *lis pendens* because he didn't pay $1.4 million in taxes, a tidy sum not recorded against title. Is a machine going to resuscitate that deal and convince the buyer to stay in contract while the legal issues are sorted out between the husband and wife?

- In late August of 2008, the buyer agrees to a fair market price for a home. On September 14, 2008, two weeks before the closing, Lehman Brothers declares bankruptcy and the financial markets crash. The home loses 25 percent of its value overnight. Can a machine articulately negotiate with the listing agent a new price that reflects the market change?

- Days before closing, a seller discloses that he didn't get the permits for work that was done, and the buyer has the right to legally walk away from the deal due to this being a new disclosure. How does a machine navigate the complexity of bringing the buyer back to the table so that the house closes escrow and permits are brought current?

There is so much unanticipated complexity, sometimes even hourly, in a residential transaction, that it is virtually impossible to guess at the complexities that will arise during any deal. While I believe that technology will make the sales process dramatically more efficient, agents will be needed to manage the process to make sure you did not leave money on the table.

Look at the history of Redfin, a start-up that attempted to disrupt real estate by being a low-cost, do-it-yourself brokerage when it launched in 2004. The company wanted to lower real estate transaction costs by eliminating the middlemen, the agents. In theory, it fit right in with the zeitgeist of technology-driven disintermediation, but there was a big hitch. People didn't like it. Buyers and sellers handling the biggest investment of their lifetimes wanted an agent to walk them through the complex buying process. Over the following ten years, Redfin pivoted to become a more traditional brokerage where an agent guides buyers through the entire sale. The company went public in 2017.

Regardless of what form the residential real estate market takes, this is for certain: Consumers will never relinquish the transparency and information they now have at a push of a button. As more and more data becomes available, buyers and sellers will increasing rely on hard numbers and public market knowledge to confirm their decision to buy or sell a home.

But data is not enough. Empowered buyers and sellers need to understand not just the mechanics, but the art, of home sales. Big data and technology will not obviate the need to appropriately prepare a home with the "right" finishes and finest staging that buyers will pay a seller a lot more for. Big data and technology cannot really grasp the multitude of local market dynamics that drive decisions on how to optimize a home sale in that specific location. Big data and technology will be challenged to understand the nuances of local markets, and how those markets approach pricing a home, to ensure that the seller ends up with the very highest price the market can bear. Big data and technology cannot provide the same level of negotiating skills that a very qualified agent with long-standing relationships can provide. Most importantly, big data and technology cannot navigate the myriad of unanticipated and often very compromising situations that happen during the course of an escrow. Those situations can and do cost sellers a lot of money, or, even worse, can result in the loss of a sale altogether. Big data and technology also cannot provide the same guidance and necessary insight for buyers on how to make the very best investment decision. Big data and technology can provide greater levels of efficiency, and certainly expedite the flow of information, but will never ensure that you have made the very best financial decision for what may well be your biggest asset: your home.

# About the Author

R aised in Marin County, California, Tracy graduated from UC Berkeley and quickly ascended in the broadcast journalism world. She worked for eight years as a reporter/anchor for various NBC affiliates around the country before hosting and producing her own tv show called *Jeep's Inside Skiing*. Tracy was licensed to practice real estate in 1996 and quickly became one of the top producing agents in her region.

In 2006, Tracy founded Morgan Lane, a boutique real estate brokerage in Marin County, California. In 2009, she and Mark McLaughlin bought Pacific Union International, one of California's largest brokerages. Tracy helped brand, recruit for, and grow the brokerage before selling her interest in it. Pacific Union became the fifth largest brokerage in the United States and was more recently acquired by Compass. Tracy has provided guidance and expertise on over four hundred homes for her clients to help optimize their resale value and has flipped over twenty-five homes for her own personal portfolio. Tracy has consistently ranked in the top seventy-five agents in the United States. She has been the single top producing agent in Marin County every single year since 2005: a record-breaking achievement. Tracy has three children and is a very active, visible member of her communities.

**TRACY MCLAUGHLIN**

# Endnotes

1   Zillow analysis of the Federal Reserve Board's Survey of Consumer Finances, 2013, the latest data available as of September 2017.

2   National Association of Realtors. "Quick Real Estate Statistics," https://www.nar.realtor/research-and-statistics/quick-real-estate-statistics.

3   Lane, Ben. HousingWire. "Zillow: Total value of U.S. housing reaches all-time high," www.housingwire.com/articles/38852-zillow-total-value-of-us-housing-reaches-all-time-high.

Rugaber, Christopher S. *Chicago Tribune.* "Americans' net worth up 1.4 percent to $94.8 trillion," https://www.chicagotribune.com/business/ct-us-household-wealth-20170608-story.html.

4   Beale, Lauren. *Los Angeles Times.* "Most Americans don't trust real estate agents, poll finds," www.latimes.com/business/la-xpm-2013-nov-13-la-fi-mo-most-distrust-real-estate-agents-20131113-story.html.

5   JP Morgan Chase. " 'Fear of Missing Out' Mindset Changing Outlook for Homebuyers," https://www.jpmorganchase.com/corporate/news/pr/outlook-for-homebuyers.htm.

6   Encyclopedia Britannica, www.britannica.com/science/Dunning-Kruger-effect.

7   Kahneman, Daniel, Jack L. Knetsch, and Richard H. Thaler (1990). "Experimental Tests of the Endowment Effect and the Coase Theorem." *Journal of Political Economy* 98 (6): 1325–1348.

Hanemann, W. Michael (1991). "Willingness to Pay and Willingness to Accept: How Much Can They Differ? Reply." *American Economic Review* 81 (3): 635–647.

8   Wolf, James R., Hal R. Arkes, and Waleed A. Muhanna (2008). "The Power of Touch: An Examination of the Effect of Duration of Physical Contact on the Valuation of Objects." *Judgement and Decision Making* 3 (6): 476-482.

9   Windsor, Callan, Gianni La Cava, and James Hansen. Reserve Bank of Australia. "Home Price Beliefs in Australia," www.rba.gov.au/publications/rdp/2014/pdf/rdp2014-04.pdf.

10  Lusardi, Annamaria and Olivia S. Mitchell (2014). "The Economic Importance of Financial Literacy: Theory and Evidence." *Journal of Economic Literature* 52 (1): 5–44.

11 Mian, Atif, Kamalesh Rao, and Amir Sufi. Semantic Scholar. "Household Balance Sheets, Consumption, and the Economic Slump," pdfs. semanticscholar.org/75a5/00894c5ffa5f9203a7e223e3a61f9eb7aa29.pdf.

12 Zillow, "Zestimate," https://www.zillow.com/zestimate/#acc.

13 A study by TCU assigned a 5–8 percent value to view.

14 Behe, Bridget, J. Hardy, Susan Barton, J. Brooker, Rodney Fernandez, Charles Hall, J. Hicks, R. Hinson, Patricia Knight, R. Mcniel, Thomas Page, D. Rowe, Charles Safley, R. Schutzki, *Journal of Environmental Horticulture*. "Landscape Plant Material, Size, and Design Sophistication Increase Perceived Home Value," www.researchgate.net/publication/232607158_Landscape_Plant_Material_Size_and_Design_Sophistication_Increase_Perceived_Home_Value.

15 Liberatore, Stacy. *The Daily Mail*. "First impressions really DO last," https://www.dailymail.co.uk/sciencetech/article-3984128/First-impressions-really-Researchers-judge-people-seen-photograph-six-months-later.html.

Gigerenzer, Gerd. *Gut Feelings: The Intelligence of the Unconscious*. Penguin, 2008.

Gladwell, Malcom. *Blink: The Power of Thinking without Thinking*. Back Bay Books. 2007.

16 Bank of Montreal. "BMO Psychology of House Hunting Report," https://newsroom.bmo.com/2013-05-02-BMO-Psychology-of-House-Hunting-Report-Home-Buyers-Visited-an-Average-of-10-Homes-Before-Buying.

17 Seiler, Michael J., Poornima Madhavan, and Molly Liechty. *Journal of Real Estate Research*. "Toward an Understanding of Real Estate Homebuyer Internet Search Behavior," https://pages.jh.edu/jrer/papers/pdf/past/vol34n02/04.211_242.pdf.

18 National Association of Realtors, "2013 Community Preference Survey," https://www.nar.realtor/articles/2013-community-preference-survey.

19 TomTom. "San Francisco Traffic," www.tomtom.com/en_gb/traffic-index/san-francisco-traffic.

20 Freddie Mac. "Home Valuation Code of Conduct," www.freddiemac.com/singlefamily/pdf/122308_valuationcodeofconduct.pdf.

21  The definition of market value is based on Fannie Mae's definition taken directly from the FNMA form 1004 URAR that appraisers use for conventional mortgage lending purposes.

22  Simonsohn, Uri and Dan Ariely. SSRN. "When Rational Sellers Face Non-Rational Buyers," ssrn.com/abstract=722484 or http://dx.doi.org/10.2139/ssrn.722484

23  Sipola, Chris. Zillow. "The Price of Overpricing," https://www.zillow.com/research/overpricing-impacts-time-market-12476.

24  Tversky, Amos and Daniel Kahneman. *Science*. "Judgment under Uncertainty: Heuristics and Biases," https://science.sciencemag.org/content/185/4157/1124.

25  Bucchianeri, Grace W. and Julia A. Minson. *Journal of Economic Behavior & Organization*. "A homeowner's dilemma: Anchoring in residential real estate transactions," https://www.sciencedirect.com/science/article/abs/pii/S016726811300019X.

26  National Association of Realtors. "The Digital House Hunt," https://www.nar.realtor/sites/default/files/documents/Study-Digital-House-Hunt-2013-01_1.pdf.

27  Beracha, Eli and Michael J. Seiler. *Journal of Housing Research*. "The Effect of Pricing Strategy on Home Selection and Transaction Prices," www.jstor.org/stable/24861816?seq=1.

28  Camacho, Christin. Redfin. "Really? Data Shows Selling a Home in Winter Pays Off," https://www.redfin.com/blog/why-winter-is-the-hottest-time-to-sell-your-home/#.VjKYm2SrTKI.

29  Stern, Mark Joseph. Slate. "Neural Nostalgia," slate.com/technology/2014/08/musical-nostalgia-the-psychology-and-neuroscience-for-song-preference-and-the-reminiscence-bump.html.

30  Carlisle, Patrick. Bay Area Market Reports. "30+ Years of Housing Market Cycles in the San Francisco Bay Area," www.bayareamarketreports.com/trend/3-recessions-2-bubbles-and-a-baby.

31  Bay Area Market Reports. "Marin County Home Prices & Market Trends," www.bayareamarketreports.com/trend/marin-county-real-estate-market-report.

32 Institute for Housing Studies at DePaul University. "The impact of lock-in effects on housing turnover," www.housingstudies.org/releases/impact-lock-effects-housing-turnover.

33 National Association of Realtors. "Home Staging Decreases Time on the Market," www.nar.realtor/newsroom/home-staging-decreases-time-on-the-market-finds-realtors-report.

34 United States Census Bureau. "Characteristics of New Housing," www.census.gov/construction/chars.

35 Bretz, Lauren. Zillow. "Quiz: Which Paint Colors Help Your House Sell for More?" www.zillow.com/research/paint-colors-help-sell-20240.

36 Mass.gov. "Massachusetts law about real estate," www.mass.gov/info-details/massachusetts-law-about-real-estate.

37 State of California Department of Real Estate. "Disclosures in Real Estate Property Transactions," https://www.dre.ca.gov/files/pdf/re6.pdf.

38 Slepian, M. L., J. S. Chun, and M.F. Mason (2017). "The experience of secrecy." *Journal of Personality and Social Psychology*, 113 (1): 1–33.

39 National Association of Realtors. "Realtors Confidence Index," www.nar.realtor/research-and-statistics/research-reports/realtors-confidence-index.

40 Burt, Fred. YouTube. "Steve Jobs Oldie but Goodie," https://www.youtube.com/watch?time_continue=5&v=vmG9jzCHtSQ.

41 Murray, Peter Noel. *Psychology Today*. "How Emotions Influence What We Buy," www.psychologytoday.com/us/blog/inside-the-consumer-mind/201302/how-emotions-influence-what-we-buy.

42 Didion, Joan. *The White Album*. Farrar, Straus and Giroux, 2009.

43 Aaker, Jennifer. Lean In. "How to Use Stories to Win Over Others," leanin.org/education/harnessing-the-power-of-stories.

44 Damasio, Antonio. *Descartes' Error*. Penguin, 2005.

45 Lerner, Jennifer S., Ye Li, Piercarlo Valdesolo, and Karim Kassam. Harvard Scholar. "Emotion and Decision Making," scholar.harvard.edu/files/jenniferlerner/files/annual_review_manuscript_june_16_final.final_.pdf.

46   Bailey, Michael, Ruiqing Cao, Theresa Kuchler, and Johannes Stroebel. SSRN. "The Economic Effects of Social Networks: Evidence from the Housing Market," ssrn.com/abstract=2753881.

47   Nielsen. "Global Consumers' Trust in 'Earned' Advertising Grows in Importance," www.nielsen.com/us/en/press-room/2012/nielsen-global-consumers-trust-in-earned-advertising-grows.html.

48   American Society of Home Inspectors. "What is a home inspection?" www.homeinspector.org/FAQs-on-Inspection#1.

49   Kahneman, Daniel and Amos Tversky. *Econometrica*. "Prospect Theory: An Analysis of Decision under Risk," www.its.caltech.edu/~camerer/Ec101/ProspectTheory.pdf.

50   Savills. "World real estate accounts for 60% of all mainstream assets," www.savills.co.uk/insight-and-opinion/savills-news/198559-0/world-real-estate-accounts-for-60--of-all-mainstream-assets.

51   Pew Research Center. "Millennials," www.pewresearch.org/topics/millennials.

52   UNC Kenan-Flagler Business School. "Maximizing Millennials in the Workplace," execdev.kenan-flagler.unc.edu/blog/maximizing-millennials-in-the-workplace.

53   National Association of Realtors. "Home Buyer and Seller Generational Trends Report 2017," www.nar.realtor/sites/default/files/reports/2017/2017-home-buyer-and-seller-generational-trends-03-07-2017.pdf.

54   Ramírez, Kelsey. HousingWire. "Americans say buying a home is most stressful event in modern life," www.housingwire.com/articles/46384-americans-say-buying-a-home-is-most-stressful-event-in-modern-life.

Mango Publishing, established in 2014, publishes an eclectic list of books by diverse authors—both new and established voices—on topics ranging from business, personal growth, women's empowerment, LGBTQ studies, health, and spirituality to history, popular culture, time management, decluttering, lifestyle, mental wellness, aging, and sustainable living. We were recently named 2019's #1 fastest-growing independent publisher by *Publishers Weekly*. Our success is driven by our main goal, which is to publish high-quality books that will entertain readers as well as make a positive difference in their lives.

Our readers are our most important resource; we value your input, suggestions, and ideas. We'd love to hear from you—after all, we are publishing books for you!

Please stay in touch with us and follow us at:

Facebook: Mango Publishing
Twitter: @MangoPublishing
Instagram: @MangoPublishing
LinkedIn: Mango Publishing
Pinterest: Mango Publishing

Sign up for our newsletter at www.mangopublishinggroup.com and receive a free book!

Join us on Mango's journey to reinvent publishing, one book at a time.